NO TIME FOR SERGEANTS

MAC HYMAN

No Time
For Sergeants

RANDOM HOUSE

NEW YORK

TO WILLIAM BLACKBURN

"This is definitely a violation of regulations."
General Mark Clark's comment
on the prisoner uprising in Korea.

NO TIME FOR SERGEANTS

1

The thing was, we had gone fishing that day and Pa had wore himself out with it the way he usually did when he went fishing. I mean he went at it pretty hard and called the fish all sorts of names—he lost one pretty nice one and hopped up in the boat and banged the pole down in the water which was about enough to scare a big-sized alligator away, much less a fish, and he spent most of the afternoon after that cussing and ranting at everything that happened. And all he caught was one catfish which warnt much bigger than the worm he was using, and he got finned by that, so by the time I brought the boat back in, he was setting in the front with the back of his neck red and his jaws moving in and out, the way he gets when he is upset, not speaking to me at all.

So after we walked the four miles back to the house, he didnt care to eat right then, so he set down on the porch and pulled his hat down over his eyes and leaned his head back against the post to doze a bit which I've seen him do for as long as four hours on the straight sometimes. So I seen he was settled for a while and I got out my harp and begun playing a few pieces. And in a little bit, he was snoring and his foot was patting up and down in time to the tune I was playing, so I played a fast one and watched it bounce a bit, and then a slow one to calm him down again—anyhow, I

was kind of enjoying it as it was quiet by that time; it was about sundown and the dogs was laying around the yard only opening their eyes every once in a while to make sure one of them didnt get fed before the other one, and the chickens was clucking easy and comfortable about the yard, and the fields across the way were kind of pink-colored the way they get sometimes when the sun is going down, so I was kind of enjoying the quiet and all, and taking it real easy that way, when all of a sudden I seen my dog Blue raise up his head and perk his ears and set there a minute, and then stare at me with this real puzzled *look* on his face.

Well, I wouldnt have thought nothing of it if it had of been any other dog, but Blue warnt the kind of dog that ever looked puzzled about anything much. I mean he was one of the smartest dogs I ever seen in my life and pretty stuck-up about it too—like when he points a bird for you, he makes out it warnt *nothing* for him to do and acts kind of casual about it and all and watches you with this real disgusted look on his face—I mean I dont guess he had ever come right out and showed he was puzzled about anything much before in his life before then.

So I really couldnt figger it for a minute. I stopped playing and listened and didnt hear nothing at first, and it was a few seconds before I made it out myself. What it was, was this far off moaning sound somewhere, and then it come to me what was bothering Blue because it sounded like a *car* to me. So I knowed why he was puzzled then because I dont guess he has seen no moren two cars in his whole life and they was more like wagons than they was cars, and I guess you might as well say that one of them *was* a wagon because this one that my uncle had didnt have no motor in it and he usually just hitched a mule to the front to pull it along, and

a lot of folks would probably think it was just a wagon, and especially a *dog* would. So Blue must have thought it was a motorboat or something and couldnt figger what it was doing coming from that direction as the river was way down behind the house and there warnt nothing in front but a road, and not much of a road at that, only some weeds with ruts on either side, and he had sense enough to know that no boat would be coming down *that* way; so he was right puzzled about it all right.

Anyhow, the sound kept getting louder and the other dogs started whining and looking around at me, and the chickens begun trotting this way and that like they do when a storm is coming up, and I stood up on the lookout for it. Then it sounded like it was almost roaring, and about that time it heaved into sight around the edge of the woods. And you should have heered the racket set up then. The dogs got to barking and howling and the chickens started squawking, running this way and that, and then the car come busting up in front of the place with dust behind it in long billows, turning and heading right toward the house like it was aimed for it. Blue took off for the woods with most of the hounds running ducktailed behind him, barking and looking back over their shoulders; the chickens went around in circles trying to dodge it, which was probably as good a way as any with the car wobbling the way it was; they darted here and there, only most of them never made any headway at all and got knocked aside and went fluttering off, all but one that went straight up in the air and came down on the hood and set there right calm for a second, thinking she had got out of the way of it, but then turning and seeing the *house* heading for her, and setting up about twice as much of a ruckus about that.

So it was pretty much of a surprise to me too because for a minute there it looked like the car warnt going to stop at all. I mean it come heading right for us and didnt begin to stop until it was about thirty feet from the porch; and then it jolted with dust blowing up past it, and stopped, and jumped forward again and finally come to a halt, and then the door slammed and this little, fat, found-faced fellow come walking through the cloud of dust talking just as hard as he could. I mean that's just the way he done too. All you could hear was the door slam and see him coming through the dust with his mouth going. You couldnt hear what he was *saying*, though—all you could hear was sounds and see his mouth moving because there was so much racket all around, and it really was surprising. I mean it looked like he was raving somehow—he was either doing that or preaching and it didnt seem natural to me that a fellow would come riding up in a car that way and jump out and start preaching even though I did know one fellow who used to jump at you from behind the bushes and start preaching—but it didnt seem that way somehow; and with all the racket going on, you couldnt tell what he was doing.

Anyhow, Pa usually warnt in so good a humor when he woke up easy and casual—I mean it usually took him a half hour or so to manage it and he warnt in much of a humor *then;* and waking up with dogs barking and chickens howling and a man stomping up and talking that way was pretty much of a shock to him any way you look at it. I seen his eyes blinking and his jaws moving before he was halfway up; then he stood there a second, shaking his head trying to get his bearings, and looking down at the fellow like he hadnt ever seen anything like him in his life before. And all this time the man kept on talking—I caught the words ". . .

want to see Will Stockdale; now is that you or aint it because
I've been riding for . . ." but that was all I could make out
—but he kept on with it, and then he raised one finger up
and started wiggling it at me, saying something else, but
about that time Pa lit into him with about the only thing
he could think of at the time, I guess, being half-asleep the
way he was; he yelled out, "Dont you pint your finger in my
boy's face!"

So that kind of stopped the fellow for a second; he turned
and looked at Pa and Pa's face turned a little redder, and
then he bellowed it out again, "Dont you pint your finger in
my boy's face!" which should have quieted him down for a
while, only it didnt, because the next thing I knowed, there
he was telling Pa he just ought to keep out of the whole
thing, that he was there to see me and not him, and that it
warnt Pa's business.

"Not my business?" Pa said. "Just what in the hell do you
mean by that, sir?"

"Look," the fellow said. "I came out here to see this boy
and I . . ."

"Just what do you mean, not my business," Pa said to him;
and for a minute he was leaned so far over him, it looked
like he might just fall right on top of him.

But then the fellow come back with something else, and
Pa kept coming back at him. The fellow was trying to tell
what he wanted to see me about and I got right curious, only
he never got to finish because all Pa could talk about was
him going around pointing his finger in my face, and it
warnt much of an argument with both of them talking about
different things that way and all.

But finally Pa out-yelled him and got him onto his argument, but then the fellow said that it was his finger and my

7

face and it was his business where he pointed it, and Pa come back with, "Not on my property, it aint," and then the fellow got off the point again and said if he had property like ourn, he sho wouldnt go around bragging about it, and then Pa come back by saying, "I dont care about that but one thing I aint going to stand for as long as I am a man is having somebody going around pinting their fingers in people's faces on my property," which was a pretty long thing to say in one bellow and left him so wore out he was kind of gasping before he finished.

But then the other fellow managed to get in a few more words, and he said, "Look, I dont care nothing about all that and I didnt come out here to talk to you nohow. I'm from the draft board and I'm out here to see this boy and that's our business and . . ."

"By God, on my property . . ." Pa said.

"That aint got nothing to do with it," the man said. "If this boy knows what's good for him, he'll get in that car right now and head back to town with me and we wont have any more trouble about it. You folks out here think just because you live ten thousand miles from town, you dont have to do things like anybody else, but I'm here to tell you different. I've been over roads that aint even been discovered yet and down trails that nothing but a horse and wagon has been down, and this is the third time I've tried to find this place, and I mean it's the last time too!"

And he kept on like that for a pretty good while and kept Pa from busting in again, but then he said, "I've wrote you four letters and havent had an answer to none of them and you neednt say you cant read neither because you could have got somebody to read them to you, so that aint no excuse!" which was about the most *foolish* thing he could have said,

8

it seemed like to me, because Pa warnt going to take that from nobody.

And he didnt neither. He drawed himself up real quick with his eyes all lit up and looked down on the fellow and just bellowed out at him, "By God, sir, do you mean to stand here and say to my face that my son cant *read!*"

"Now look," the fellow said.

"Do you mean to come busting up here and not say Howdy or nothing and say my son cant *read* and expect him to go hopping in that car like you said? Do you think my son who has gone to school and has read more times than you could shake a stick at couldnt answer a puny little ole letter if he wanted to? By God, man, let me tell you . . ."

"All right," the fellow said. "Then there aint any excuse at all for him not answering them letters . . ."

"Letter?" Pa said. "By God, sir, I dont think I can stand to listen to any more of this . . ."

"Well, that's all right with me. Now . . ."

"Nosir!" Pa said. "What you think dont mean nothing to me, but I'm going to make you eat them words just the same. Will, you go in the house and get that book and lets see about this thing here and now and not have no more foolishness about it."

And he stood there with his arms folded and his mouth clamped together, so there warnt nothing much I could do but go get it; and when I got back, he hadnt budged, so I set down on the steps and opened it up. Then Pa said, "Go ahead, Will," without even looking at me, and so I read him a couple of pages out of it. It was about this little boy named Tony who wanted a pony and how he went to work for a man so he could buy it, but he never made enough money, so the man finally just *give* it to him because he

9

worked so hard. But I never got to the end of it because Pa raised up his hand all of a sudden, and I stopped, and he lowered his hand and said, "All right, that's enough of that one. Now go in and get the Bible and let's hear a few of them words in there."

"Now look, I dont care anything about that," the fellow said. "I . . ."

"Go on, Will," Pa said. "I want to get this here thing straightened out once and for all, by God."

So I went in and got the Bible and when I come back out, Pa still had his arms folded, so I set back down on the steps and give him a dose of that one too. I read him a few lines about that fellow that warnt a nigger but was called Abraham, and I done pretty good with it, I think, only I didnt get to finish it neither because the fellow busted in again, saying, "I've had enough of all this. I'm asking you for the last time now. Are you going to get in that car and go back into Callville with me or are we going to have to come out here and get you?"

And that set Pa off again so that he done some pretty fierce cussing right up in the man's face and asked him what he *meant* by that and all; and when the fellow said, "I mean just what I say. They'll come out here and take him if he dont come with me and they can do it too!" it looked like Pa was going to tear into him all of a sudden. He rared back with his chest poking out and his face turning red and lifted his fist up and bellowed out, *"Off my property!"* so loud that the fellow's face turned right *white*. He started going backward, looking at Pa with his eyes wide, while Pa kept making these noises in his throat; and then he turned and headed for the car and slammed the door and started driv-

ing out just about as fast as he had been coming in before.

Pa was right wild by that time, too; he run around until he found himself a rock and he heaved it at the car just as it was turning off onto the road, but he missed it and hit my dog Blue instead, as Blue was just coming out of the woods about that time, so that Blue looked right at him and gave this yelp and headed back for the woods again; and by the time Pa could find another rock, the car was gone and there warnt nothing left but dust floating across the ditch.

Anyhow, after things settled down a bit, Pa was right wore out from it all. He set down on the steps to rest, looking weak and trembly all over; he kept shaking and turning white in the face and when I tried to talk with him, he didnt have nothing to say. He would just rub his hands over his face and shake his head and lean back against the post again.

But after a little bit, he begun to feel better and talk some, even though he didnt sound much like the same man as before. He shook his head and looked at the ground and spoke real soft and sad, and said how it warnt right for folks to act that way. He said it was sinful to get mad with folks too, and he felt right bad about it. He said, "Will, why dont you read a little more out of that Bible again?" and I said, "Yessir, why dont you just rest a while," and reached over and got it and read to him for a spell. He set there listening, nodding his head up and down, and I read a part with a lot of big words in it, and I done pretty good with it, I think. I throwed in a lot of Thees and Thous and Verilys and things like that, and when I hit some of the big names, I just called them Sam or Joe or whatever come into my head, but he didnt know the difference; he nodded his head up and down, looking like he felt better already. I read, "And

11

he saideth verily thee unto thou," and he cleared his throat and said, "That's the truth, too, Will. That's the truth."

So I read a little more and after a while he begun talking more about how folks ought to be good to one another and not bear false witness and not worship no false idols and stuff like that, and seemed to perk up a good bit thinking about it. He got to going about as good as most preachers until he got hungry and begun smacking his lips and wiping his mouth as he talked, so finally I said, "Why dont you just rest a while and I'll go in and get some supper ready?" Because by that time I had decided that the draft didnt sound like such a bad idea to me and I had just as soon go like the fellow said, and I wanted him kind of rested and comfortable and kind of holy feeling, the way he got when his stomach was full, so I could tell him in a kind of casual way and not get him upset no more.

So I went in and fixed up just what he liked best—grits and side meat and toast and coffee—and had it steaming on the table when I called him in. He pulled up his chair on one side and I pulled mine up on the other, and he went at it real steady because nothing makes him more hungry than getting mad; and I kept quiet most of the meal waiting for a chance to bring it up to him. He set there eating with his jaw stopping every once in a while, kind of looking off into space like he was thinking, and then starting up again when he got whatever it was that bothered him straight in his head. He cleaned up one plate and started on another and I set there sipping my coffee, and then he got up and started pacing up and down the room, his chin kind of hung down on his chest, thinking all along. He put

12

his hands behind him and walked from one end of the room to the other, nodding his head like he was talking to himself.

So I put off talking to him and cleaned off the table and stacked the dishes, waiting for him to get settled, but when I got through with that, he was still walking, only now he was going faster; and instead of having his hands behind his back, he was clenching up his fist and slapping it in the palm of his other hand and all like that, and seemed real lively and happy about everything. He paced up and down like he warnt tired at all, and sometimes it looked like he was even chuckling to himself, and when I seen that, I knowed there warnt much hope in being casual about it no more. Because if he had decided it warnt right to get mad with folks, he would get this kind of sickly, holy look on his face and his voice would get right weak, and he would talk about forgiving and so on; and you could see plain as anything he warnt feeling that way about it now. He looked too lively and happy for that; his eyes was lit up and he was just prancing around, so I knowed then that he had figured it out somehow to suit hisself and so finally I just set down in a chair and rolled a cigarette and waited for it to come.

It warnt long coming neither. Because just about time I got it lit, he turned around and looked at me and pointed his finger and said, "Will, you read the Bible, dont you? You go to church?"

"Yessir," I said.

"You think Jesus was a good man, dont you?"

"Yessir."

"Couldnt nobody do any better than to live a life like Jesus, could he?"

"I dont guess so," I said.

"So the thing is to do just what Jesus would have done, aint it?"

"Yessir," I said. "That's a good idea. Now I was thinking . . ."

"Well, do you know what He would have done?"

"Nosir, but . . ."

"Well, I do," Pa said. "I know what He would have done all right. If a man come riding up on His property and scared His chickens half to death and didnt say Howdy or nothing, and then went around saying folks couldnt read, *I* know what He would have done all right. He would have sent that man straight to *hell,* by God!"

And he stood there staring at me with his eyes lit up and his finger in the air, as full of spark as I had seen him in a mighty long time.

2

So after that, there warnt much that I could do about it. He got it in his head how he wanted to fix up the place so nobody could come busting up like that any more, and we worked half the night on it. I never seen Pa so full of plans

and things in my life neither. The first thing he wanted to do was pull out all the rolls of barbed wire we had in the barn and drag them out front and leave them in rolls on this log fence we had out there. "We'll just stack it up along here," he said. "That way a man will have a right hard time getting through it. What do you think about that, Will?"

"It sounds like a mighty good idea," I said.

"Sho," Pa said. "Come on, let's get the rest of it," and he took off for the back again, moving faster and more spry than I had seen him in many a year.

Anyhow, we worked on the fence about two hours, I guess, and both of us worked pretty hard too. I dont think I would have cared too much for it, only there was a big moon out and Pa begun singing to himself, making a kind of party out of it, and the dogs were running around real excited, and after a bit, it begun to be kind of fun. Pa went in and got a bottle and we both had a drink, and then he got to singing all the church songs he knowed with these bundles of wire over his shoulder. He sung that one about "Just a little walk with theeee!" and I come in on the chorus of it and we made a right good duet out of it. Pa had about as bad a voice as I ever heered, though, and didnt know but two notes with one of them high and the other one low, but he hopped back and forth between the two pretty good and didnt sound anywhere near as bad as usual, so it really warnt too bad. We finished laying out the bundles along the fence, and then Pa got the idea of stringing what he had left from tree to tree out in the woods, just about the level of the grass, so that a man coming along might trip over it. So we done that on both sides of the house, working about another hour at it, I guess, and I thought Pa had really outdone himself in thinking of things to do, but then he got the idea of tying

the dogs out there to the trees so they could set up a howl if they heered somebody coming, and that took a little while to do because the dogs didnt quite recognize Pa with him singing and taking on the way he was and wouldnt come any-where *near* him. He had to chase the only one he caught by running around the house about three times behind him, and only managed it then by diving headlong after him, which almost scared the poor dog to death. But we finally managed to get them all but Blue and we never could get him because he never did come back out of the woods no more. We seen him every once in a while, setting behind a bush with his head poked around the side, watching every-thing, but he never would come out no more, so finally we just had to give him up for good.

Anyhow, I thought that would be enough for Pa, but he was sweating and happy and still hadnt tired none, and he said, "Will, this is one time we can get some good out of them chickens," and then told me another idea he had about catching them all too and stringing them up by one foot to the bushes out in the woods and using them as kind of watch-dogs too.

"Well, that sounds like a mighty good idea," I said. "But it'll take a pretty long time catching and tying up them chickens and we been at this about three hours now and . . ."

"That dont matter," Pa said. "We got all night, aint we? Come on, lets have one more drink and get down to it now."

So we started on that, chasing the chickens around the yard with them squawking and flapping their wings in your face and making noises like you were wringing their necks. And I really was kind of surprised that Pa got through that one because he never really cared for chickens nohow, and

16

one of the big ones got right on his shoulder and beat his wings over his face and pecked at him until he fell in one of the bundles of wire one time, so that it took me nearly a half hour to get him out of it. But it didnt stop him neither; he went right on until we had them all out, and they worked even better than I thought they would. We had them tied by one foot so they wouldnt get tangled up, and when we finished and went over to the well for a drink of water, I threw a rock down in the woods and you never heered such barking and howling and yelping in your life. There aint any more ungodly yell that I know of nohow than a chicken yelping when it's scared—it's louder than a dog any time, especially way in the night like that—and you have to give Pa credit for it all right; he had really outdone himself.

Anyhow, we stood around and cooled off and put a dipper of water over our heads, and I was right wore out with it all. But I guess by then I was about as wrapped up in the thing as Pa was because I got the idea myself about how we should go down and tear down the bridge along the road so no cars could come up it, and I was just ready to mention it when I remembered I warnt really too much for it nohow. So I didnt say nothing about it, but kind of got to worrying that *Pa* would think of it. But after a little while, he said, "Well, I guess that is about as good as we can get it," and I said right quick, "Yessir, I reckon that pretty well does it."

Then Pa said, "I want you to know that I appreciate you helping me out and everything; hit would have been a lot of work for one man to do." And then he stood there a minute looking around the place, waiting for me to say something.

So I caught on and said, "Well, sir, I was mighty glad to do it," and then I said, "I appreciate *you* helping *me* out."

17

But he shook his head and said, "No, Will, you was doing it just to be nice. I know hit dont make no difference to you, but I want you to know I appreciate it."

So then I said that warnt so at all. I said, "Nosir, you got it all wrong. I feel just like you do. If they come riding up here, I'll blow their heads off. You just see if I dont."

But then he shook his head sideways at me and smiled kind of sad, and said, "No, Will, the only reason you'll blow their heads off is because you're so good-natured. But I do want you to know I appreciate it."

So I didnt say no more about it. He had his head set on it that way, and I guess when you come right down to it, it was the truth too. So I let it drop and tried to change the subject. I said, "I wonder what happened to them letters the man was talking about."

"I dont know," Pa said. "I guess they must have just come in down to the Corners and they forgot to give them to us. I dont think I would tell them that, though. They would just think you couldnt read and didnt want to say so. Some people think that way, you know."

So I said I would be sho not to mention it and we stood around a while longer, and I throwed another rock down in the woods to try the chickens and the dogs again, and they set up a pretty good racket again, and once they quieted down, we went on in to bed. I was dog-tired too and slept hard all night long and didnt wake up until after the sun had come up the next morning when I heered Pa fooling around with the stuff in the kitchen.

3

The thing was, I guess, I had kind of halfway expected Pa to forget all about it once the fun of it was over, but he hadnt at all. He already had breakfast fixed when I got up, and while I was eating, he got out this twelve-gauge double-barrel shotgun he had, and then he got out a rifle and this other gun that's been around the house as long as I can remember, and he took them out on the porch and started loading them up. I went ahead and washed the dishes and when I come out he was just loading the long one. It had one of them large hammers on it and the barrel was bent, and you had to load it by stuffing powder down the barrel, but Pa liked it, and I've seen him hit things with that old bent-barreled gun that you could never think of hitting with no other gun.

Anyhow, he finally finished with it, stuffing nails and everything else down inside it, and then loaded the others, and after that we set there and waited, and I got right tired of it too after a while. I mean I didnt mind going to the draft much nohow and it seemed like we was going to a good bit of trouble about nothing to me. I didnt say nothing *about* it, of course—Pa was so touchy about things like that—but it really did seem that way to me, and I had to do a good bit of things to keep from telling him what I thought about it. I played the harp a while and raked up around the front

19

while he set there next to the post with the gun across his lap; then I went out and watered the chickens and the dogs that was tied up, and then we both set around for a couple of hours, and I really did get right tired of it all before it was over.

I mean waiting around like that not knowing whether you're going to have to blow somebody's head off or not can be right *wearing* after a while. And they didn't show up until nearly noontime nohow, and by that time, it really did seem like it was all more trouble than it was *worth* to me.

But the waiting warnt nothing to all that happened after they got there. What happened was, we were both standing there when these three cars come driving up—we had heered them whanging over the bridge down the way—but they didnt see us at first because they were leaning their heads out the window looking at the rolls of wire we had rolled up in the front. They were setting there with the motors still running, pointing at it and talking about it.

And it was about that time that I seen Pa's gun coming up. It's the longest gun you've ever seen in your life, and it come up and up and finally hung out there in the air with him sighting down it and looking like it was pointed about forty feet in front of the first car so that I almost expected them to start laughing at it the way I've seen some folks do when he aims at something with it, because by looking at the barrel you cant tell which way the shot is going. But Pa knowed all right, and I did, and I'll bet if he had of pulled that trigger then, he would have hit the man driving the first car within about half an inch of where he had decided he would hit him.

Anyhow, what happened was that it just caused another big ruckus. One of them looked up and seen Pa and give a

holler to the others, and they come piling out of the cars all of a sudden, doors flying open and heads ducking down, scurrying all over the place. And they kept yelling at each other and all like that, peeping over the sides of the cars and things; and this one fellow, I thought he never *would* quiet down. What happened to him was, he was right fat and when he tried to get out, he got stuck in the door on the side toward the house, and hung there, jerking and snatching around and hollering his *head* off. And I guess he never would have stopped, only he looked up finally to see Pa sighting at him; then he stared a second and quit yelling and just hung there, like he was dead sure enough and there warnt a thing he could do about it.

Anyhow, there were eleven of them in all that I had counted, not counting the fat fellow because he didnt amount to so much, and the next thing I knowed, there I was trying to figger out which one to shoot first. I mean I didnt *want* to shoot nobody, and I didnt mind the draft neither, but I was all primed up for it all of a sudden because of all the noise and everything, so I went ahead and throwed a shell in the chamber of the rifle and started getting lined up for it. And when I seen this arm come up from behind one of the cars and seen the handkerchief waving, I drawed down on it right quick, waving the gun back and forth, not even knowing what was going on for a minute.

But then Pa called out, "All right, Roy, come on up!" and yelled it so loud that it made me jump and almost pull down on the trigger I was so primed for it and everything. But I stopped myself right quick and looked at Pa and then recognized it was Roy Burton he was yelling at, and I lowered the gun and stood there watching him as he come walking up to the wire, standing there looking at it. I remember

everything seemed like it was all mixed up all of a sudden. I was so pitched up for it that it made me feel kind of shaky and let down and sickly somehow.

But then it come to me right quick that that was all it was, it was over just as quick as it had started. I could go on in and get my stuff and go in to the draft, and that was all there was to it. It made me feel mighty good all of a sudden and I turned to Pa, but just about that time, he called out, "What do you want, Roy?" and it hit me then that they was going to start talking some more, and I mean it made me feel ornery too. I mean I just didnt care to fool with it no more.

But then Roy called out, "I want to talk to you, Tom. Can I come up there?"

"Shore, Roy, come on up."

"How'm I gonna get there, Tom? You speck me to crawl under this here wire?"

"I reckon it's the only way, Roy," Pa called back. "If you want to come up here."

So they talked some more that way for a while, and I finally just set down on the steps and put my rifle across my lap and tried to keep my mouth shut until they got it straightened out, one way or the other, it didnt matter to me much any more.

Anyhow, they talked back and forth, and Pa said Roy would have to come through the wire or not come at all, and then Roy tried to wiggle through, but he got all tangled up; and then they had to call back and forth for a while to get somebody to come out and help him out, only that didnt work too good because didnt nobody want to come out. So Roy called up and wanted Pa to vow not to shoot one of them if they did come out, but Pa said, "I couldnt vow that, Roy;

one of them might take it in his head to cause some trouble and then I'd have to break my word." But he finally decided he would let one man come up if he left his gun behind, and they kept pushing this fellow out but he kept going back behind the car again, so finally they got this other one to come out, only that didnt do no good neither because he got hung up in the wire just like Roy did. So finally the only thing left to do was to go back and get the clippers. Course Pa could have walked out to the wire, but he wouldnt do nothing like that—no, if they wanted to talk to *him,* they would have to come up to where *he* was. So finally I went out and clipped Roy out and talked with the fat fellow for a bit; he said it was right hot and I allowed it were and such things as that with him still hanging there in the door, and then we talked about crops for a while, but finally I got Roy out and followed him up to the porch to talk with Pa.

Roy used to live out at the Corners and him and Pa knowed each other and it seemed like to me they could have got it straightened out right quick, but then they had to argue about it a while just the same. McKinney, the one who was out yesterday, come and stood in front of the car and called out things for Roy and Roy called back to him, and then him and Pa talked about it a while. And what it come down to after about ten minutes of that was that McKinney wanted me to get in the car and go back in town with them, and Pa said he had already made it clear what he thought about that and warnt going to back down on it. Then Roy called out, "Hey, McKinney, he says Will can come in all right but he aint going to ride in. How about that?"

Then McKinney called back, "We came out here to get him and that's what we're going to do. We want him to come in right now."

Then Roy turned to Pa and said, "What's the difference, Tom, if he comes in now or later on? I dont see nothing wrong with it."

"Nosir," Pa said. "I've made up my mind about that and there aint going to be no changing it."

So they went on that way a good while until I kind of got on McKinney's side of the argument because I didn't mind riding back in the car nohow. But they kept yelling back and forth that way until what it come down to was that *Pa* thought it would be all right for me to come in as long as I *walked* in, and *McKinney* finally said it didnt make no difference to him *how* I got there, just so long as I *got* there. So actually McKinney finally backed down on the thing. I didnt see much sense in him giving in that way and really thought the less of him for doing so, too.

But anyhow, both of them said they was going to stand on that and there wouldnt be no more change about it, and they called back and forth a little bit longer with both of them getting staunchier and staunchier about it, until after a while they had it all settled that way. And then Roy shook hands with Pa and then Pa walked out to the wire and a couple of them came over to shake hands with him, and then Roy went over and shook hands with McKinney, and some of the others did too, and then there was a big to-do about getting Pa and McKinney to shake hands with everybody patting everybody else on the back and everything. So I watched a while and finally went out to shake hands with somebody myself, but about that time they started getting in their cars, waving and everything, and I kind of hated to see them go. I hadnt rid in a new car in my life, I dont think, and I didnt care a thing about having to walk no twenty-seven miles into Callville when there were three cars headed right that

way, but I never said anything about it. I guess it was better me walking than having people getting their heads blowed off all over the place, so I never mentioned it; I went on out and started untying the dogs and chickens and getting up the wire and things.

The way it was, I was supposed to be down at the courthouse in Callville before five o'clock that afternoon and so I had started out just as the sun was coming up because it was a pretty long way and I knowed I would have to keep at it steady to make it by that time. I had fixed me some biscuits and meat in a sack so I wouldn't have to waste no time stopping to eat, and I figgered to stop by the Corners for a drink and then head on to town. They had a store there with cold drinks and things and an old pool table in the back, and a gas tank outside, so there was a chance that I might catch a ride on in the rest of the way. But that morning there warnt any cars or wagons there. There warnt nothing but two men setting on the front playing checkers and two others standing around watching, and some hens strutting around, and some dogs, so I went on in and got me a big grape drink

and set on the steps outside and et my biscuits and meat and rested. And then I talked with the fellow that runs the place a few minutes, and by that time it was nearly eleven o'clock, so I got up and was just ready to head into town when I seen Bart Glovers coming up the road.

I seen him and he seen me, and he was a good way down the road, but I would have knowed him a mile off, I guess. I started to go back in the store and out the back and circle on around and maybe miss him that way, but there warnt no chance in it; he had already begun waving his hands at me, so I stood there on the steps waiting for him and waved back. Then he waved some more and begun trotting a bit and come up to the store grinning with his teeth poking out the way they do, bobbing his head up and down. It warnt that I didnt want to see him; I had knowed him a good while, but I was in a hurry and didn't have the time to fool with him. He stuttered a good bit and he was real touchy about it and always had the idea in his head that didnt nobody want to talk to him none because he stuttered and didnt nobody like him for it, and he kept on about it all the time until it was pretty near the truth. But there warnt nothing I could do, so when he come up whooping and hollering, I whooped and hollered back, and he punched me in the stomach and I messed up his hair a little bit and then he begun kicking at me some and then we rassled around a little bit, and before it was over, I was right glad I had run into him after all. I hadnt seen him in a long time but me and him used to go hunting together a good bit and I always liked him fine for a little bit at a time, only he was hard to stay around for long because he was so awfully ignorant and so touchy and all over his stuttering; but anyhow we rassled around a little bit, and

then he stood back blinking his eyes real hard the way he does and said, "Well, I be danged, Will."

And I said, "I aint seen you in a coon's age."

And he said, "What in the dog are you doing here?" grinning and blinking his eyes at me. "I be danged. I sure as danged didnt expect to see you." That was the way he took on all the time. He was the worst fellow at trying to cuss I ever did see and I guess he'd been at it for ten years and still hadnt learned. I mean he would say things like, "What in the dog are you doing here?" and never know it made no sense at all. But that was the best he could do and I never did hold it against him none because I had known him a long time and I could make out what he was getting at most of the time anyhow.

I said, "You old devil, you."

And he said, "You old dang," and we hit each other a few more times; and then we went on talking about this and that until he asked me what I was doing, and I told him about the draft and all, and he got real excited about that. "Are you really, Will?" he said. "How is it they ever come to ask you?"

So I told him how it was, and he stood there blinking his eyes a little bit, so I could tell he was trying to figger out why it was they asked me, and didnt ask him. Then he asked me who it was that wanted me for the draft, and I told him it was some fellow named McKinney, and then he begun nodding his head up and down. "I know 'em," he said. "He's the one, huh? I'll tell you about him sometimes. Me and him dont get along so good."

"How do you know him?"

"Didn't you know? I been living in town for about two years now."

So I asked him what all he had been doing and had he

been doing any hunting lately and why hadnt he been out to see us and all like that, and finally he perked up some and we talked of this and that, and after a little while, he said why didnt we go in and shoot a game of pool. Well, I started to say I didnt have the time, but I seen he was watching me and blinking his eyes, and then I knowed I would pretty much *have* to shoot one with him. Because if I had said something about being in a hurry because of the draft, he would have thought I was throwing that up in his face, and wouldnt have liked it none. So I said I would. It seemed like the best thing I could do was just shoot a quick one and get it over with that way.

And that ought to have been easy enough on the table they had. It was setting in the back of the store along with a bunch of feed sacks and it had these big ridges in it and wore out places going right toward the pockets so you had to be practically blind not to make two or three balls on it every time you shot, and it warnt no trick at all to run the whole table with about four shots, so there ought not to have been nothing to it. But Bart didnt shoot pool like most people you've seen. He made a pretty big thing out of it and was always talking about it taking brains to do this and brains to do that, and made out it was the main thing about pool too, and I guess he done it because he was so ignorant; and he always has to figger and measure, and everybody has to be quiet and all like that. He gets down and eyes along the balls and he wont do it just to the cue ball neither—he gets on the *other* side of the table and eyes them from that direction too.

So I seen soon enough it warnt possible to shoot no *quick* game with him. I busted them up and he started getting lined up for his first shot and he was even worse at it than he used to be. I guess it took him nearly fifteen minutes to get

around to shooting. He eyed around and then he felt the weight of all the cues and then he went around testing the bounce of the cushions with his finger everywhere he ex-pected the ball to hit; and then he stared at the table for a while, and leaned over real slow aiming, and then he got up and shook his head and went over and set down on a bench next to the table and started rolling himself a cigarette. And then he set there, studying it some more, and smoked most of the cigarette up, still staring at the table, and then he got up and measured some more, and I thought he never *would* shoot. And when he finally did get around to it, he had figgered it out somehow that he was going to hit three different sides of the table before hitting the ball he was after; and of course that warnt even possible on a table that had ridges in it about half as deep as the ball; so, even though I wouldnt have believed that nobody could shoot on that table without making at least two balls, he managed to bound all over it and not even *hit* one.

I knowed what I had to do then, though. I knowed if I run all the balls on the next shot, he would just want to shoot another game, and he would keep on that way until he had won one himself, which could have taken all *day* the way he shot, so I figgered the easiest thing to do was go ahead and make sure he won that first one so he would be satisfied, and I could head on into town. But I found out that was a pretty hard thing to do on that table. I mean if you just come within an inch of a ball and the breeze wobbled it going by, it would roll over and get in one of those gullies and head straight for the pocket like it had a string on it. So I started trying to figger a way so I wouldnt make a ball, and I never shot such a game in my life. I got to figgering just about as hard as he did. I had to figger the

gullies and the ridges and all like that, and before I got off my next shot, I was about all wore out with it. But I managed not to make a ball and felt pretty good about it, and then it was his time and we had to wait around another fifteen minutes for that one. Anyhow, we went on that way for over an hour, I guess, before Bart finally come fanning close enough to one of the balls to set up a little breeze and blow it down one of the gullies to the pocket, and after that he got right cocky and shot without figgering no more than a couple of minutes, and run the whole table on me.

I was mighty glad to see it too. I got up and put up my cue and told him he was just too much for me and I warnt going to take him on again without a lot more practice, and it worked out all right. He kind of chuckled and took on and patted me on the back and tried to cuss a little bit but got it all messed up so it come out, "I hell nearly missed that last ball, didnt I, Will?"

Anyhow, I still figgered I could make it by running a mile and walking a mile, but when I was ready to start out, Bart said, "Well, I'm ready any time you is," and I mean that kind of got me. Because I guess Bart was about as slow as any man I ever seen when it come to walking. He didnt really walk nohow. What he done was kind of lean forward until it looked like he couldnt stay up no longer without falling on his face and then his legs started moving to keep him from going down, but they was the only part of him that *did* move. His arms just dangled straight down by his side and his head bobbed up and down, and it looked like the only way he ever got from one place to another was just by pointing himself in that direction and leaning forward until his legs started moving, and *falling* his way there.

Anyhow, it was past noon when we finally got going. I

tried to hurry him up some but he tired right easy and he always had to stop and look at things along the way something like a dog stops and sniffs, and we didnt make much time no matter how I prodded him. One time we run up a covey of quail out of the ditch along the side of the road and they fluttered up and lighted back in some wire grass, and wouldnt nothing do then but we go out and try to point them. That was one thing Bart could do pretty good, though, and he was right proud of it, and I couldnt blame him much about it. Course, he had practiced on it a good bit but it warnt all just practice—I think myself that he had about as good a nose on him as anybody I ever seen because I've seen him point just like a bird dog with his eyes closed, and not many people can do that if they practice all their life on it.

Anyhow, he said he had been in town so long that he didnt know whether he could do it any more or not and wanted to see if he still could, and he got down on his knees and closed his eyes and raised his head up, sniffing the air, and then begun crawling through the grass with me behind him. He done pretty good too; he pointed two of them right off and knowed just how close he was and everything and didnt stir them up but held his point until I called out, "Rush, boy!" and he give a leap forward and the bird come fluttering up. It was a pretty good thing to be able to do and I guess it is about the best way I ever seen to train a bird dog. I mean you can try everything you want to with a dog and he might not point right, or might not hold his point and things like that, but then you get Bart out there and let him get down that way and go sniffing along until he gets a scent, and then point and everything the way he does, and I mean it *does* something for a dog. I've seen dogs that never was the same afterward, once they seen Bart do that.

Anyhow, we wasted a good bit of time that way because I got interested in it because I always have liked to watch Bart smell out quail, and I nearly forgot the time. But when I did think about it, I made it right clear to Bart that I had to be getting on into town, and for the next three or four miles, we made some pretty good time. But then he got wore out with the pace and when we passed this mule and wagon along the road, wouldnt nothing do but we hitch a ride for a while for him to get rested up. There was an old gray-headed nigger driving it and he said we could go along and we got on, but I dont think I ever seen anything slower in my life. I guess the mule was about as old as the nigger was, and they looked something alike too, and we just barely moved along, it seemed like. So after I decided I couldnt stand it no longer, I got down, and told Bart, "You just ride on in if you want to, why dont you? I'll see you in town later on."

But he come climbing down right after me and followed along because by that time he had decided to go see about the draft himself. He said, "I sure as dog dont see how come they aint said nothing to me about it, do you? It's that fellow McKinney, I think. We aint ever got along so good." And after a little while, he had his head so set on it that there warnt a chance on earth of trying to talk him out of it.

He said he was going right in and ask McKinney why they didnt ask him too and he was going to get an answer one way or the other. He begun blinking his eyes talking about it, and kept on with it until I begun to feel right bad about it myself. I didnt figger there was a chance in the world he would ever make it, though. He couldnt read and that was probably the reason they hadnt asked him in the first place, but course I couldnt tell him that. If I had, he would have gone around after that telling everybody I was bragging and

32

everything, and never would have forgive me for it. So I didnt say nothing, but just listened to him fussing about it, and agreed with him that they hadnt acted right to keep him from feeling any worse about it than he already did.

The more he thought about it, though, the more he blamed McKinney, and before we got to town, he was good and mad about it. He took on about it and cussed and ranted, or at least tried to cuss and rant, but he warnt no good at it, but anyhow he flipped his teeth up and down and talked real loud, and I couldnt calm him down a bit. So when we got there and it was nearly dark and we seen that the court-house was all closed up, I didnt feel too bad about it because it didnt seem like we would get to see McKinney nohow. I said, "Well, Bart, looks like aint nobody here. I didnt quite make it after all."

But then he said, "You just come with me, Will. I know right where he lives. Dont you worry about it. I'll tell him why you're late and I'll fix it up so I can go along too. Dont you worry about it."

And then I think he kind of halfway got it in his head that McKinney had gone and closed down the office just be-cause he knowed he was coming by, and that made him all the madder. He come about as close to real cussing about that time as I ever heered him. He took off stomping down the courthouse steps, heading down the street waving his hands and taking on, and there warnt a thing I could do with him except follow him along and calm him down as best I could. It was dark and the street lights had come on, and he kept trying to find the house; we went down this one street and Bart stopped and said, "No, I believe it is up this way," and then he turned and went up that way, and then stopped and said, "No, it's down yonder, I think," and was

off again looking from house to house. And then he decided it was on the other block and we went over there but we couldnt find it there neither, only he thought he had one time and went up and banged on this door, yelling, "McKinney, you come out here," except that it warnt McKinney at all, but a little old man with glasses on who locked the door and turned out all the lights and peered out the window at us.

So then we went back to the first block again, and this time Bart stopped and looked at the house across the street and said, "By hell, Will, there it is right there. We done passed by it two times."

"Well, look," I said. "Why dont we . . ." but he was already headed across the street, moving fastern I ever seen him go before, leaning so far over that his legs just went lickity split trying to keep up with him. He stomped up the steps and drawed his fist back and went to beating on the door so that you could hear the windows rattling. Then you could hear people inside jumping up and running around the house, and calling to each other, and some women saying, "What on earth, what on earth." And then Bart opened his mouth to bellow, only it warnt much of a bellow because he got to stuttering right in the middle of it, and said, "McKinney, you come out hyer or I'm coming in and b-b-bring you out b-by your *ha-ha-hair!*"

You could hear it all up and down the street, too. I heered some doors open and seen people sticking their heads out, and then Bart took to beating on the door again. And about that time, the light went out inside the house and I seen McKinney running across the living room to the front door where he turned the lock, and then running back again. And all that time this woman was going, "What on earth,"

and Bart kept on beating and yelling, "By your *ha-ha-hair!*"

You couldnt do a thing with him. I said, "Bart, come on. You can see him tomorrow maybe," but he banged away on the door again and said, "By dog, dont you hear me?" and wouldnt quit for nothing.

I said, "He aint coming to the door, Bart. Why dont me and you just go on and maybe you can come in the draft later on."

But he wouldnt budge; he kept beating away and rattling the door until he got tired of it, and then he went over and set down on the steps, shaking his head and saying, "No-sir. Me and him never got along nohow and this is the last hell straw."

So I finally just set down there with him, thinking he might sooner or later remember somebody in some other part of town that he was mad with, but we hadnt been there no time when this car come down the street with its spotlight shining up in the yards and everywhere, going real slow, and I knowed it was the police time I seen them. But Bart still wouldnt move, so we watched them stop and then seen them hopping out around the sides of it, both of them with their pistols out already, and it made me feel right ornery watching. I mean it looked like everywhere I went, folks were jumping out of cars pointing guns at people, and you get kind of *tired* of that after a while.

And then somebody inside the house put on the porch light and there we sat with the spotlight from the car on us and up the walk come the policemen with their guns out and everything, and it was right wearing. They come striding up saying, "What's going on here?" and then McKinney came out of the door, and there *he* was toting a gun too with his eyes real big, and all the neighbors was standing out on their

porches watching; so I just moved aside and tried not to listen to it any more.

The police knowed Bart right off, though. When they seen him, one of them said, "It's him again. I told you so, didn't I? Didnt I? Didnt I tell you so?" and the other one shook his head and said, "Aw, come on, Bart, what are you doing now?"

So then Bart started trying to tell them what all McKinney had done, and then McKinney busted in telling them what all Bart had done, and they argued about it a good bit. McKinney said he wanted Bart locked up and he didnt mean maybe; and then the policeman got right mad too, only he said he didnt want to lock Bart up because he had just let him out last week. He said, "Now, Mac, I just aint going to do it. We've had him up there four times in the last two months and he just lays around and eats moren any four mules you ever seen—by God, Mac, I just cant *afford* to keep him up there no longer. I got other prisoners to think of and they aint going to put up with it much longer neither and I cant say I much blame them."

Then Bart busted in again saying he just dared them to try to take him in, and then McKinney said, "Listen to that, will you?" and the policeman said, "Yeah, that's what I *am* listening to and if I take him up there, that's what I'll *have* to listen to for the next two months, and I got a wife and family living downstairs in that jail, Mac, and it just aint fair of you to expect me to take him back in there no more."

Anyhow, they was arguing so hard that there is a chance McKinney never would have seen me because I was setting back in the dark, but about that time the other policeman looked around and said, "What about him?" and then the

older policeman saw me and said, "Yeah, that's it! Now we'll take him in, Mac, if you want us to, but this other fellow, I . . ."

So then McKinney seen me and I mean that really set him off. His eyes got big and he backed off and then he stepped up again getting red in the face, and before it was over, he was taking on worse than he did the first day he come out to the place. He told the police that I was that Stockdale boy and that I was the draft-dodger that was supposed to report today and didnt do it, and more things than I ever heered before. I finally stood up, and he begun pointing his finger at me again and raving around, and the policeman kept nodding his head up and down, listening and smiling, saying, "Yeah, that's it, Mac. He's the *one* all right. Let's lock *him* up and let this other one go."

"I want them both locked up," McKinney said. "I tell you he's dangerous and I know."

"Well, let's lock *him* up because he's the one that . . ."

"Nosir," McKinney said. "I mean *both* of them."

So they argued about it some more, and McKinney held to the point. He said, "You let him out first thing in the morning and see that he's in front of the courthouse at seven sharp. I dont want him left around town here at all. I want *him* on that bus in the morning."

So they finally decided to do that, and it was all right by me. In the morning I would get on the bus and it would give me a place to stay that night besides. And then Bart spoke up and said if that's the way it was, he would go along to jail after all. He said he was going to stick with me all the way. He took on a good bit that way going out to the car, and I kind of appreciated all the things he said, but I was tired and hungry and really didnt care too much one way or the other.

And to tell the truth about it, I didnt look forward too much having to spend the night with Bart nohow, knowing there warnt no way of getting away from him. I really couldnt much blame the way the policeman felt about him at all.

But Bart acted real nice once they got us back to the jail. He showed me around and seen that I got the best bed and introduced me to everybody, and seen to it that we got something to eat and everything. It just went to show what a good friend he could be if he liked you, and I appreciated it too because I was right tired and my feet was aching and I was kind of wore out with things anyhow. Because when you come right down to it, I didnt care so much about the draft in the first place.

5

Anyhow, I got up real early the next morning and dressed waiting for them to let me out, thinking I might have a good chance of getting out before Bart woke up, but the sun was already up when they come after me. But they didnt have no trouble with Bart at all, it seemed like, once I was ready to go. He acted real nice and didn't raise a ruckus or anything and seemed right satisfied to be right where he was. It's that

way with a lot of folks though—when they're doing what they want to do, they are just as nice as they can be. And I dont guess Bart had ever found a place in his life that suited him as much as that jail did; he just didnt seem like the same person somehow.

When I was ready to go, though, they decided I had better have a guard go with me and they got this little fellow that come up to about my shoulders to go along. The courthouse was only half a block from the jail, but this fellow was right nervous and jumpy and wanted to walk behind me and all like that. He kept good guard all right, but his lips was trembling the whole time and he kept jumping and jerking everytime I moved, and after a while he begun to make me kind of nervous too. I mean I had to watch myself and move real easy to keep him from getting any more upset and all. When we got to the courthouse steps, I set down real slow, and when I started to roll a cigarette, I was careful about that too, and I had to talk in practically a whisper, so I begun to get right anxious for the others to show up so we could get on the bus and go.

Anyhow, they started coming up a little after that, dribbling up in twos and threes and standing around on the steps smoking and talking to each other. I nodded at the first few that came up and would have spoke if they had nodded back, but didnt none of them do it; they just went over and stood amongst each other. They seemed like a right nice bunch, though—the only thing was, I dont guess it made such a good impression on them because I had this *guard* with me. And they was mostly town boys and knowed each other, and they was dressed alike in their spotted shirts with the tails hanging out and these slick-looking pants and things, and I still had on my khakis and brogans; so I didnt let it bother

39

me none. I figgered we would get along all right once they seen that fellow warnt much of a guard at all, so I didnt push it none. I set there and smoked and watched them come up, some of them in cars that their folks drove, waving good-bye and all like that, and then standing around joking with each other and all. And there was one of them I watched a good bit because he seemed kind of different from the others and stuck out, so to speak. I mean he kind of stood away from the others and was real quiet and had these dark glasses on and held his back real straight, and he didnt go around punching at everybody like the others did. He would just look at them real serious when they came over to speak to him, and then he would kind of nod his head a little bit, like he was thinking of something else; and then he might mumble something and they would all stop and listen and wait for him to say something else. But then he usually wouldnt—he would turn his head away again and take a big drag on his cigarette and blow it out real smooth and steady, kind of twisting his head around to look at something across the street.

So I watched him and heered them calling him "Irvin" and tried to figger him out. I didnt have no luck at it, though, until I heered this one fellow say to somebody else, "That fellow's had ROTC," or something like that. Anyhow, I didnt know what it was because I never had heered of it before, but then I heered this other fellow mention the same thing and see how impressed they was by it, so I finally figgered that he must still have a touch of it in him. I mean I got to thinking that at one time or another, he must have almost died from it. So they seemed like a real nice bunch the way they made on over him and everything, and I kind of admired ˙t the way he acted too. He didnt ask anything

from nobody but stood there just as straight as he could like he could take care of himself no matter what.

Anyhow, in a little bit, McKinney come walking up, and was grinning and taking on real merry with everybody himself, and acting real nice about everything. He said, "Well, you boys go up there and show them the kind of men we raise down here," and they all joked back at him; and then he said a lot of funny things like, "Dont take any wooden nickels," and "Dont do nothing that I wouldnt do," and "Be good, and if you cant be good, be careful," and a lot of things like that. Course he didnt speak to me or nothing, but he did seem a lot nicer once you seen him being friendly that way.

And then he done something else I thought was real nice of him too. He went over and patted Irvin on the back and said, "Irvin, I want you to keep these boys in line now. I'm leaving you in charge of them for the rest of the way, you hear?"

And Irvin nodded his head, just as casual as he always was, and said, "Okay, McKinney," like it didnt mean a thing to him. He kind of took a deep drag on his cigarette and then held it between his fingers and flipped it out in the street, like if they wanted to make him head man, that was up to them, and he hadnt asked for it all.

So I thought it was a pretty decent thing for McKinney to do, but about that time McKinney kind of tapped him on the shoulder and said, "Come over here a minute. I got a few things I think I better tell you before I leave here," kind of cocking his eye at me when he said it. And then he got Irvin over to the side and got right up in his face and talked and talked, looking over at me every once in a while. And then Irvin would kind of glance back over his shoulder at me and

then nod his head again, and then McKinney would get to going again. And in a few minutes there was three or four of them ganged around listening with their heads popping around at me and then back at McKinney again; so I seen then he warnt putting no half-dead man in charge just to be *decent*. He was just *using* him. Once I figgered I warnt going to stand for it no more, but time I made a move to get up, I heered the guard suck in his breath real deep and I looked around at him and he was right white in the face, so I set down again.

So I didnt do nothing, and then McKinney got out in front of them and made a little speech, saying as how Irvin was in charge and for everybody to do just what he said and all like that, and then he said "Good luck" to everybody and raised up two fingers and went on off down the street. And then everybody got to joking around again, and then Irvin got out in front and made a speech too about how he expected everybody to behave and how he was going to assign seats to everybody and all like that. So then they joked some more and took on a good bit, and there was this one fellow called Lucky that kept everybody laughing all the time. When Irvin said he was going to assign seats to everybody, this fellow said, "Well, I got a seat all right but I just got to find a place to put it," and everybody laughed a good bit about that one. He told it a few more times, and then he told the fellow next to him, "I want a seat for my seat," and said a lot of crazy things like that that just kept everybody laughing all the time.

So I kind of got to enjoying it and nearly forgot about McKinney, and when I seen Irvin heading over toward me, I nodded my head and smiled real pleasant at him. And I stood up too, even though it did make the guard jump. But

then Irvin walked right up to me and said pretty rough, "Stockdale, I dont want any trouble out of you, you understand that? I dont want one peep out of you. You get on that bus and sit down dont open your mouth until we get out. You might as well start learning something right now—when you're in the Army, you do as you're told."

"Sho, I will, Irvin. Whatever you say."

"My name to you is Blanchard," he said.

"Oh," I said. "Well, whatever you say . . . I'll do whatever you say." It did kind of get away with me, though, because I had been smiling so pleasant when he lit into me that way.

And then he kind of cocked his head to one side and looked at me kind of funny and said, "You aint trying to get smart with me, are you?"

"No, I aint . . . I just want to tell you about McKinney. He . . ."

"Well, dont," he said, and then started to turn away and walk off, but then he stopped and said, "And I thought you was so tough . . ." but then he caught himself and said, "Not one peep, you understand?"

And I said, "Whatever you say . . ." and set back down because by that time he had walked on off and I didnt have a chance to explain nothing to him.

So then I set back down and everybody went over and crowded around Irvin asking him all sorts of questions and things. And after that they kind of started making remarks at me. They kind of held back at first until Irvin stepped up and said kind of short, "Hey, boy, you aint planning to go AWOL, are you?"

So I looked up and said, "What's that?" and he come back with, "You wouldnt know if you went, would you?" Then

everybody kind of laughed, and then come ganging around, and *all* of them got started on me. I mean they would ask me things like had I ever been in town before, and had I ever rode in a bus before, and things like that. And then Lucky asked if I had rocks in the bottom of my shoes to make me think I was barefooted, and everybody laughed and hee-hawed about that one, and I did too because I thought it was right good; but then they got rougher and rougher, so I got where finally I wouldnt say nothing at all. I mean Irvin was standing there and he was in charge and all, and I warnt going to cause him no trouble if I could help it. So finally I just wouldnt say nothing and set there smoking like I didnt even hear them. So they let me alone for a while, but when the bus come up, Irvin give me a shove and said, "Let's get moving there, boy," and that kind of set them all off again.

But anyhow, I kind of enjoyed the trip up there. I got me a seat in the back of the bus and after a while they sort of forgot about me and I got a kick out of it. I had been to Pinehurst but that was as far north as I had ever been, but that day we went right on through Pinehurst and come to another town just as big, and then another one that was as big as Call-ville and Pinehurst put together, I bet. And in a couple of hours we went through Macon and I bet it took us half an hour to even get through the place. Then after Macon there were some more towns and looked like we never would quit going through them all. Anyhow, I really enjoyed it that way but somewhere between Macon and Atlanta, I dozed off and didnt wake up again until we was finally at Fort Thompson.

Anyhow, I must have been sleeping pretty hard at the time. I remember I was dreaming about fishing down on the creek and all of a sudden this moccasin come skimming across the

water and bit me right on the leg. It really made me hop because the pain was running all through it and when I come to and seen Irvin and all the others standing there over me, it was just like *he* was the snake and had changed into a man all of a sudden. So I started at him before I knowed what I was doing. I reached out and snatched him by the neck so he almost come over the seat, and then I swung him around and was just ready to bust him one before I come to and knowed what I was doing. And of course it was too late by that time, and I felt like a dog mighty quick, too. I hadnt hit him, but I had scared him a good bit there for a minute and I felt pretty low about it.

And he got pretty mad about it when he seen I warnt going to hit him, and I didnt blame him at all. He cussed me right through his teeth with his eyes squenched up and when he got through cussing me every way he could think of, he drawed back and give me another good kick in the shins. I had it coming too. I reached down and rubbed it and said, "I'm sorry, Irvin. I guess I didnt know what I was doing or something," and humbled myself a good bit that way.

And after that, I set out under a tree waiting for us to go wherever we was going and didnt nobody say nothing to me for a good while. They was all kidding around and making on over Irvin for the way he tied into me, and I was kind of glad to see it too. I felt so low treating him the way I had that I was glad to see any good he could get out of it. All I could do was cuss myself and wonder if I could ever get things straightened out again after the way I had started off, and get along in the draft, and not have no trouble, and just get along with everybody from then on.

6

Anyhow, they finally took us down to this place that had a lot of bunks in it, and I went down to the end to get away from the rest of them and set down on the bottom bunk and rolled me a cigarette and was just getting ready to light it when this scrawny little fellow with big glasses on walked right up to where I was setting and stood there looking at me. He didn't say nothing, just stood there, and when I looked up to see who it was, I seen it warnt none of the bunch that had come up with me. He was real little and he had on this uniform that was so new it still had the sideways creases in it, and he had on one of them little half-hats that are supposed to set on the side of your head, only his set all the way down on his head and come almost to his eyes. And the pants he had on was mighty near long enough for me—he had them rolled up about a foot off the floor—and he had on this coat with brass buttons that looked too big for him to even be *toting*. And besides that, he had this bag over his shoulder that you could have put four of him in, and he stood there looking at me with the sweat rolling down the side of his face, looking right miserable, so I knowed right off I hadnt seen him before; and the first thing I wanted to do was to jump up and help him with it all.

But he kept standing there looking at me, and then he tried to grin, only he couldnt manage it so good because the

46

bag pulled him so hard on one side that it seemed to pull his mouth sideways too, but anyhow he tried, so I set up a little bit and said, "Howdy."

He still kept looking at me, and then said, "How are you?"

"Just fine. You well, I hope."

And he said, "Yeah, I'm okay," and kept standing there looking at me until I said, "Right hot, aint it?" because he looked like he had fell in a creek or something with all those wool clothes on the way he was sweating; but then he said, "Was you going to take that bottom bunk?"

"Was this yourn?"

And he said, "Well, not exactly. But usually in the Army, it's first come, first served, and I was here . . ."

"Sho," I said. "Sho. You go right ahead and take it. I didnt know you . . ."

"I should have left something on it to show it," he said. "That's what I should have done. But I didnt do it. It serves me right, I guess. I should have knowed better."

"You can have it," I told him. "I was just setting here."

But he shook his head and said, "No, you go ahead and take it. I should have left something. It was my mistake."

"I'd just as soon . . ."

But he kept shaking his head. "No, it was all my mistake and I should have left something and I dont deserve it for not knowing better."

So he had me kind of bothered about it then and I tried to argue him into taking the bottom one anyhow, but he kept shaking his head and wouldnt hear nothing of it. So then I told a big lie about how I couldnt stand sleeping next to the floor nohow and how at home I always heisted my bed up about five feet off the floor with brickbats under it and had to use a chair to crawl up in it, but he just kept shak-

ing his head, saying, "No, anybody in the Army ought to have sense enough to leave something to show what was his," and acted like he didnt care to talk about it no more.

And then he started trying to chunk his bag up on the top bunk but he couldnt get it up much higher than his shoulder, grunting and puffing with his face turning red. I wanted to help him, but being little and scrawny the way he was, I knowed he would want to do it all by himself so I just stood back and let him heave at it a while until I seen he warnt likely to make it, and then I said, "Looka here now, I'd ruther have that top one, and I mean it."

But he shook his head and heaved again and said, "I'm gonna take it."

"No, you aint," I said. "I said I wanted it and I do, and I aint gonna take no for an answer."

But he kept on trying to hoist his bag up there, so I give that up and finally edged around the side and got one hand on the bag to give him a lift without him knowing it; but about that time Irvin come bounding across the room saying, "Get your hand off that bag, Stockdale. Let the man alone. I stood just about as much as I'm going to out of you."

So I took my hand off it right quick and it was too much for the little fellow. The bag fell and mighty near knocked him over so I had to catch him to keep him from going down. And then some of the others started crowding around to see what was going on, and I said, "Irvin, I just . . ." but then he started lighting into me again. And it looked like he got rougher every time with it too; and this time he got started on me saying I thought I was so tough and yet didnt do nothing but pick on fellows half my size. "Cant you find anybody your own size to pick on?" he said.

"Look, Irvin, I didnt mean nothing. I . . ."

But then the little fellow got into it himself. He snatched himself up real straight and looked Irvin right in the face and said, "You watch your mouth!" And it kind of got Irvin a second too. He looked at the little fellow and started to say something else, but then the little one pulled himself up straighter and said, "Why dont you mind your own business anyhow?"

"I was just trying to do you a favor, fellow," Irvin said. "This fellow tries to . . ."

"That's between him and me," the little one said. "No-body asked you to butt in."

"Now look, I was just trying to help you out, Shorty. I was just . . ."

And that one really set the little one off. "Who are you calling Shorty?" he yelled out. "Who asked you anything anyhow?"

"All right, if that's the way you feel about it. If that's the way you want to be, you be that way."

"Well, that's the way," the little one said. "Just keep out of things that dont concern you."

It really got Irvin's goat too, having him talk at him that way. He looked kind of puzzled and started to say something else, but couldnt think of anything to say, so finally all he done was turn around at me again and squench up his eyes and say, "If I have any more trouble out of you, I'm going to let you know about it, fellow," and turn and go stomping off to his bunk on the other side of the room.

The little one was hopping mad, though. He kept mumbling to himself and pushing around at the bag and everything and I felt pretty good about the way it come out. I knowed I should have tipped him off somehow about Irvin but I didnt have the chance, and to tell you the truth, I

didnt care much anyhow. I set down on the bunk and watched him until he finally got the bag up on the top one and then stepped back trying to breathe easy so it would look like it warnt nothing for him to do to be tossing the bag up that way. I said, "You want a cigarette?" but he shook his head and started to say something, but then had to wait until he got his breath back, so I looked the other way like I didnt notice it, and then he said, "I dont smoke. It takes your wind away to smoke. Thanks just the same, though."

And then I said kind of low so nobody else could hear, I said, "I guess I should have told you before but I didn't have no chance—Irvin has had ROTC. I didnt figger you knowed it. I heered it myself just before we left home."

"That dont make any difference," he said.

"Well, he must have had it pretty bad," I said. "The way they talked . . ."

"What do you mean, pretty bad? It dont make any difference how much he had of it—if he didn't finish the course and then go ahead and take the Army course afterwards he dont rank any higher than anybody else. As far as that goes, he aint even been swore in yet and even when he does, he wont be no higher than the rest of us because they dont give out any rank in ROTC until you finish the course. He might act like he has all the rank there is, but I know better. I guess I know how ROTC works all right. I've read four or five of them ROTC manuals and I know what it amounts to . . ."

I listened to him talking about the ROTC and he had to keep going for a good while before it ever come clear to me, but course I wouldnt let on none about it then, I just kept my mouth shut and let him run on about it, and I got to feeling dumber and dumber, and then I begun to feel right good about it too. I looked over to where Irvin was setting on

his bunk talking to Lucky and some of the others, and in a minute I was feeling right happy about it too. And I dont guess I could have picked a better one to tell me about it than the little one because he seemed to know more about it than the ROTC theirselves. He knowed how it started and when it started and all like that, and he said he had a cousin that had Cavalry ROTC at the University of Georgia and he knowed another fellow that had Infantry at Dahlonega, and then he started telling me the difference between the two and how he like the Infantry better because they was the real soldiers, and the others warnt nothing but helpers, and all like that. He was down on the others a good bit too, it seemed like, especially the navy. He didnt like them at all. "You just think about it," he said. "Little old white uniforms and walking around on boats and things all the time. You just think about it."

"Yeah, that's what I always thought," I said. "The Infantry is the best one."

"There just aint any comparison," he said. "Listen, what about the War between the States? What about that?"

"Yeah," I said. "That's what I always thought too. What about that?"

"That's what I always say," he said. "You see what I mean?" Then he looked over to where Irvin was setting and said, "I'll bet he aint had no moren a year of it, if that much. And it was probably Cavalry or Field Artillery or something like that. I bet it was Field Artillery."

"Well, it dont do him no good here," I said.

"That's right. He aint no more than we are."

"That's right," I said. "He sho aint. He aint no different from nobody else."

And the more I thought about it, the better I felt. There

I was feeling like a dog for grabbing at him the way I done, and there warnt nothing wrong with him at all. I mean it made me feel good knowing it too.

So I thought on it a while, and it was almost enough to make me mad, so I cut out thinking that way soon enough. It didnt do any good to go around fussing with folks nohow. All I wanted to do was just get along with everybody and not have no trouble, and I figgered it would work out sooner or later as long as I was friendly and didnt cause no ruckus or anything, so I made up my mind to forget it.

So when we fell out in front of the barracks and got in lines to go eat supper, I spoke to everybody real nice and tried to talk to them like nothing had happened, but they still didnt have anything to do with me. And when we got lined up, there was ole Irvin right behind me, and he kept on at me worse than ever. He'd say, "You straighten up there," and I'd work hard at it, and then he'd say, "Walk in step there, boy, you aint behind no plow now," and would stomp on my heel, and everybody would laugh and take on about it. But I didnt want no trouble and just wanted everything to be forgot, so I would kind of chuckle and take on like I thought it was about the funniest thing I ever heered. And then he'd jab me in the back and things like that, and then kick at my heels some more with everybody heehawing, and I'd try to heehaw a bit myself, only it was right hard to do with my heel hurting that way, but I heaved my shoulders up and down and made myself grin, and all like that.

So I figgered I would just laugh my head off all the time and things would get all right, but when they got started on little Ben too—that was the little one's name, Ben Whitledge —I didnt like that too much because he hadnt done nothing to nobody. And once we had set down at the table, they kept

on at both of us. I chuckled and took on the best I could like I thought they was a mighty sharp bunch all right, but they didnt let up at all. Irvin kept kicking me under the table saying, "Dont eat so sloppy, boy. You aint with hogs now," and then Lucky would come out with something like, "I'd fix him a trough but I dont think the hogs would like it," which were right funny when you come to think of it, so I did get a good chuckle out of that one, only most of them warnt that funny and I had a right hard time laughing all the time. And Ben didnt take to any of it much. He set over there, and when they called him "Glass Eye" and stuff like that, he didnt act friendly at all. He wouldnt say a word and finally he finished up and took his tray and got up from the table and left, like he didnt think any of it was funny at all.

So I tried to fix it up with Ben when I got back over to the barracks. I didnt come right out and say how he should act or nothing because I seen how stubborn he was, but I took on a good bit about how funny Irvin and Lucky was, only it didnt seem to go over with him too much. I said, "Did you hear that one Lucky said about fixing a hog trough only the hogs wouldnt eat with me?" and then I rolled back on the bed and laughed about that like I was going to die over it, but he set there polishing the brass on his belt and didnt say a word. I said, "That aint nothing, you ought to have heered some of the good ones they pulled on me on the way up here," and I heehawed about them some, and then I said something about the way he stomped down on my heels and all, and heaved my shoulders up and down over that one. Only I couldnt really put out on that one because I kept remembering how my heel hurt, but anyhow I chuckled and took on a good while, and he didnt pay no attention

to me at all. He finally just got up and started getting undressed and mumbled to himself, "Well, they just better keep away from me, anyhow."

But I didnt know what else to do so I kept on with it trying to be friendly all that next day. But you couldnt change Ben none much, he was so stubborn that way, so I tried to do for both of us. I giggled and took on like a fool about everything they said to me, and when we got down to the place where they shot you with the needles and they started saying to the medic, "That fellow says you cant hurt him, mister. He says you cant even get it in his arm," and got the medic in on it too so that he jabbed it nearly all the way up to the hilt, I took on like it was the biggest joke I ever heered of. I laughed and rubbed my arm and said, "Yall sho fixed me up that time. Yessir, I'm sho gonna get you back for that one—hee, hee, hee." and I laughed some more, and kept trying to wink at Ben. But every time one of them would say anything a little bit out of the way to him, he would turn on them in a second, and when one of them called him "Shorty," I really thought once or twice he was going to bust them one.

But I kept at it all day until my mouth was froze in a grin and it didnt do no good at all. The more I giggled and took on, the more they found to do, and before it was over even Ben wouldnt speak to me much.

So I seen after a while that something would have to be done. It looked like they just warnt going to let up on neither one of us, and Ben warnt liking it neither. So I set down on the bunk and rolled me a cigarette and tried to figger out what to do. I reckon if it hadnt of been for Ben, I could have worked it out by laughing my head off all the time, but he was the stubbornest little devil I ever did see.

He set there polishing his belt and stuff, never saying a word to me. And to tell you the truth, I was getting right tired of it *myself,* when you come right down to it.

So what I finally decided was that the only thing I could do was just go ahead and bust some of them a few times. I didnt want to, but the laughing warnt doing no good and Ben was getting the wrong end of it and all like that, and I really didnt feel I had much choice in the matter. So anyhow, that's what I decided I would do.

So what I done, I waited around until after supper and then I went back to the barracks and waited for the chance to come. I mean it wouldnt make no sense to just start *banging* away at them, so I set around waiting for somebody to say something to me. Ben was laying up in his bunk reading and I kept waiting around for a while, but nobody come up. So then I begun singing a little bit, thinking somebody would say something about that, but nobody did, so I cut that out and got up and walked up and down the barracks, bumping into their beds where they was reading or sleeping, stumbling here and there trying to make a racket, and I did get a few comments on that but not really no *good* ones that I could get upset over. So I went back and set down and smoked a cigarette and tried to think of something else to get them started. I got out my harp and blowed on it a while, blowing pretty loud and missing about every other note until it was so awful sounding that it hurt even my ears, but the only one that bothered was Ben, and he didnt really say nothing, only turned over and covered up his head with his pillow.

So I finally decided that the main ones—Irvin and Lucky and them—warnt around, and that was what the trouble was. They were all in the latrine where they had a card

game going on the floor, so that seemed my best bet and I went in there. I stepped on some of the cards going in and then I went over to the sink and turned on the water and let it splash around, singing real loud and all like that, and then I walked back by and tripped over Lucky's foot, and done a lot more things like that, but they was all pretty wrapped up in the game and I didnt get a rise out of nobody. So I stumbled around a good bit more and bumped into people and things like that, but it still didnt do no good, so finally I just give it up. I went on back to the bunk and started getting ready for bed, thinking I would just have to wait it out until they got started again.

But just about time I started getting off my clothes, Ben got up and took his soap and towel and headed for the latrine, and in a minute I heered somebody say something to him and him say something back, and then I heered all the talking and laughing and scuffling around and things. So I got up off the bunk and went real slow and easy, kind of tiptoeing back to the latrine, and when I looked in to see what they were doing, and when I seen what was going on, I figgered I couldnt have worked it out no better if I had thought on it all night long. They had Ben down under one of the sinks and had the water running ready to stick his head under it with two or three of them holding him and Ben rassling around trying to get away, and everybody yelling and everything. So it looked like a pretty good thing to bang them around for a little bit, and I felt real good about it.

I went about closing the door real easy and then I closed up the windows, and none of them seen me until I let the last window down with a bang. Then Irvin turned around and said, "Well, if it aint ole plowboy," and laughed and

took on so that the others begun to do the same. And then Irvin said, "What are you doing in here, plowboy?" and some stuff like that, but then I give him a pretty good scowl and didnt laugh or take on like a fool the way I had been doing, so I guess then they seen something was different. They kept taking on some, with Irvin still in it more than the rest of them, but I scowled real hard again and took a couple of steps toward them, but I think they really knowed better by that time. Irvin kept saying, "Look at ole plowboy," and trying to joke about it but the smile had long gone off his face and he had begun shifting his eyes this way and that. Anyhow, they let Ben go about that time, and I kept looking at Irvin until all of a sudden he drawed back real quick and said, "You better watch it, boy, there's six of us here and . . ." but he didnt get to finish because I tapped him one with my left so he quit right in the middle of it as his head popped sideways and backward and he kind of wobbled across the room and dropped over a sink and didnt get up no more for a while.

So then it looked like they was all going to make a break for it, but I managed to stop them all right, though. I grabbed the first one that got to the door by the shoulder and swung him around and busted him a pretty good one, harder than I meant to, so that he kind of sailed across the room and banged up against the wall and slid down and set there for a while. And about that time one of them climbed on my back so that I just jumped up in the air and come down on top of him and heered all the air gush out of him, and then I seen old Irvin getting back up again. So I stepped past the others real quick and swung one at his jaw, but not as hard as I had the other one because I didnt want him to be just laying there the whole time; he went back-

ward and flipped over one of the bowls and ended up in pretty much the same position he had the first time.

So after that everybody joined in just as spunky as you could ask and it turned out to be a pretty good fight after all. I went around with the others a little bit and finally hemmed a couple of them up in the corner and acted like I was going to hit one that had his face covered up with his hands, but dodged aside and hit the other one instead, and then had to chase the other one for the door again. I grabbed him by the foot and give it a snatch and he went up and banged down on his stomach and I picked him up and tried to see how far I could chunk him and managed to hit the wall on the other side of the room. But that busted one of the mirrors and made a good bit of noise, and things kind of dwindled off a bit after that. Irvin got up one more time before it was over and then another fellow got up, but there warnt much else to it, except for Lucky over in the corner and little Ben had him all by himself. He was setting right astraddle of him and was doing pretty good, so I didnt bother with it none. I set down and rolled a cigarette and smoked it until Ben had finished up with Lucky, and then both of us set around waiting for them to get up again. Little ole Ben was kind of prancing around all that time too, doing his fist in and out and taking deep breaths and things, and he had this big grin on his face, so it did make me feel a lot better. I said, "How you doing, Ben?"

And he kind of flexed his muscles, or what he had of them, and said, "Fine. Fine," and it really made me feel good to watch it. It had been a lot of trouble and some of them might be mad with me for a few days, and the place was a mess with cards and glass and cigarettes and matches all over the floor, but it seemed like it was worth it. Ben was

prancing around like he was a new man; he was just as proud as he could be and strutted around like a little bantam rooster.

Anyhow, we set around for them to get up and then opened the door and let them all go to bed, all except Irvin who still hadnt come to real good. I told a couple of them to go back and help him along, but they warnt quite up to it, so me and Ben finally had to do it ourselves. Ben warnt able to handle much more than one foot, but he done a good job with that, and we got him to bed all right. We tucked him in and then got in bed ourselves, and I felt real comfortable and a lot better, and knowed I would sleep pretty good. I hadnt had no exercise to speak of for the last day or two and it was right good to feel wore out for a change. I turned over and guess I was asleep in four or five seconds at the outside.

7

Anyhow, it turned out that everybody was pretty nice the next morning, and not really mad at all. I got up early, before Ben did, and went down to the latrine, and there was several of them in there and they acted real polite to me. They was kind of shy at first, though. When I first come in,

this fellow stopped shaving and stared at me, and I nodded "Good morning," but he just stood there with the razor in his hand and his mouth open. So I reached up to give him a pat on the back to be friendly, but time I got my arm up, he give a jump and ducked his head and dived past me, rolling up in the corner and setting there with the soap still on his face, holding onto the razor. So I seen he was right shy and eased back away from him and stepped over to one of the bowls to wash up, but then I seen this rag already there and this fat fellow by the name of Pete standing there watching me, and I said, "Oh, was this one yourn? I didnt mean to take it."

And he jumped and said, "You go ahead. I aint in any hurry."

"No, I'll wait until you finish."

"I aint in any hurry," he said.

But I stepped back and let him go ahead, and he acted mighty nice about it. He didnt take long at all, only leaned over and splashed some water on his face and grabbed up his stuff real quick and said, "There you go. I'm all done. Thanks a lot."

"Much obliged to you," I said.

So they all acted real shy and polite like that, and as friendly as you could ask. One time I mentioned something about the cards all over the floor, and before I got it half out of my mouth, there was four of them scurrying around and picking them up and straightening up the place.

Anyhow, I went ahead washing and begun whistling a little bit, and after a while some of the others sidled up next to me and took to washing too; and then I finished and went back to get Ben up. But he seemed to be sleeping mighty hard and when I shook him, he only grunted and didnt

.move. So I decided to let him rest a little longer and went over to get Irvin up; and when I got over there, I seen he didnt look so good. The side of his face was about the color of coal dust and his lip was swoll up a pretty good bit, but I knowed he would feel better if he got something to eat, so I shook him until his eyes opened. I said, "You best get up, Irvin, or you might miss breakfast," and for a minute there, I thought he was right mad with me because he just kept staring at me, and then give a little moan and closed his eyes up real tight and wouldnt even look at me except to peep out of the corner every once in a while. He didnt move until I had gone back over to get Ben up, and then he got up right quick and headed for the latrine, going right fast.

Anyhow, I kept shaking Ben and telling him he was going to be late for breakfast, but he only grunted at me. I shook him and said, "Come on, Ben. The chicken's done crowed and wants to water," and then he opened his eyes and frowned a little bit and kind of looked toward the ceiling.

"Come on," I said, because he didnt make any move to get up, just kept laying there.

"What's the matter with you?" I asked, because then I started getting worried one of them had hurt him last night. "We got to get going. It's late."

And then he rolled his head over and pushed back the covers and set up, his eyes kind of blank-looking and his hair hanging down in his face, and said, "All right. All right, I'm getting up," and climbed out of the bed without saying another word to me.

And it kind of bothered me the way he acted—the thing was, Ben warnt usually slow-moving like that. I mean usually he was running around polishing things and straighten-

ing things, so it didnt seem natural to him. He clumb out of the bed and begun putting on his shoes, moving as slow as I ever seen him; and then stood there on one foot wobbling as he put on his pants; and then picked up his soap and towel and headed back for the latrine, just kind of dragging himself along.

And he stayed back there until we was already outside getting lined up ready to go for breakfast. I kept watching the door waiting for him until I got right fidgety about it; so finally I went back inside to get him, and when I got there, he was standing back by his bunk, putting on his shirt like he had all the time in the world.

"Boy, we better get going if you want some breakfast," I told him. "I never seen you so slow."

He kept putting on his shirt, buttoning it up one little button at the time. Then he yawned and said, "I didnt sleep much last night."

"I slept good," I said. "I aint slept so good in a long time."

"I did too at first, but then I waked up and got to thinking and didnt go back to sleep for a while."

"You did?" I said. "How come you done that?"

"I dont know," he said. "I just did." Then he was about ready to say something else, but we heered them outside ready to march off about that time, and we had to start running to catch up with them.

Anyhow, we had a good breakfast and I et more than I had in a long time. I et what they give me and then Irvin couldnt do nothing but drink his coffee on account of his jaw, and I et his, and then I et some of Lucky's too that he couldnt get down, so I had a pretty good breakfast for a change. But Ben didnt hardly eat a thing. He just picked at it with his fork and busted the yellow of his egg and stirred

his coffee a lot, and all the time kept staring at his plate like it made him mad even to be there. And in a minute, he got up and took his tray and left the mess hall without saying a word to me, and went back to the barracks all by himself.

And when I got back, he was laying up in the bunk staring at the ceiling again. So I set down and didnt bother him none about it; but after a while it begun to grind at me, and when everybody had gone down to the orderly room to sign some papers, I lit a cigarette and puffed on it a bit, and then I asked him straight out what it was that was bothering him.

He kind of twisted around and said, "It aint nothing. I just didnt get much sleep."

"Did any of them hurt you last night?"

"No. No, it aint that . . . It's . . ." But then he just said, "Awww . . ." and turned his head the other way. So I waited a bit, and then he set up real quick and looked at me and said, "Will, you shouldnt have done it. You shouldnt . . ." and then stopped again, and said, "Awww . . ." and laid back down again.

"What? I shouldnt have done what?" But he kept shaking his head back and forth. "What is it I shouldnt have done, Ben? You just tell me, I'll . . ."

"It aint no use. It warnt your fault."

"I bet it was, too. I bet it was all my fault. What is it, Ben?"

"You wouldnt understand. It warnt your fault because you just didnt know any better and I didnt help none. I didnt . . . Awwww . . ."

"You tell me, Ben," I said. "I'll fix it. You tell me."

"Awww . . ." he said. "You . . ." and then he bounced

63

up again and slapped his hand on the bed and said, "Dog it, Will. Dog it," which sounded pretty powerful coming from Ben and made me jump. He said, "Dog it, Will, it might have messed up everything. Here I done come up here and kept my mouth shut and aint done a thing to nobody, and then I figgered that you and me . . . well, I didnt have no right to think it, but I thought you might be willing and I got bad eyes and thought I had it all fixed up and now . . . Will, they are *bound* to hear about it. They are just bound to."

"They what? Who?"

"Somebody's bound to tell them about last night and then what? Then what? You think they want folks in the Infantry that acts like that, Will. No sir, they dont want to have anything to do with them. They want folks what can take it and keep their mouths shut, the way a man ought to do. Oh, it warnt your fault. I done just like you did, once it got started. But it warnt right, Will, it warnt . . . A soldier dont do things like that, Will. A soldier . . . you see, a soldier, well, he dont have to go around getting in little fusses in latrines with anybody that comes along cause he just got off the battlefield where there's real fighting and what does he care about some little ole fight in a latrine when . . . See, that kind of thing's *peanuts* to him, Will, cause he's just been on the battlefield and he dont have to go around strutting and fussing . . . Dont you see, Will?"

"Well, not quite," I said. "We aint been on no . . ."

"Awww, I knowed you wouldnt understand," Ben said. "But just listen now, Will, and try. You see, they dont want little folks like that in the Infantry, and I . . . Listen, my great-grandpa was under Stonewall Jackson in the Battle of Chancellorsville and he even *knowed* him and Stonewall

give him a medal one time that I still got at home, and his brother was with Forrest, and my Dad, Will, my Dad was in the Rainbow Division, and I had two brothers in the last war and *all* of them was in the Infantry, and now suppose I dont make it because of last night. They dont want soldiers what blow up like that, you see? Now a sailor can come in in his little ole white pants and fight in latrines and act real little, but he hadnt just come off no battlefield, Will; and a man in the Air Force, he aint been right down in it and it dont make no difference with him, but a soldier, a real honest Infantry soldier that's been in *real* fighting on the battlefield . . . Look, Will, you see what I mean? You see?"

"Kind of," I said. "Except this about the battlefield, Ben . . . That dont make right good sense to me because . . ."

"I knowed you wouldnt understand. Dog it, listen, Will. Listen," and he leaned way over and looked at me and said, "They might put us in the navy and we'd have to wear them little white uniforms, or they might even put us in the Coast Guard or the Air Force . . . Will, do you know what they call men in the Air Force?"

"No, I dont think I heered say."

"They call 'em . . ." and he waited a minute and kind of twisted his face and said, "They call 'em *airmen*. By dog, Will, dont you see? How'd you like to be called an *airman?*"

"By God, I just dont think I'd stand for it . . ."

"You'd have to!" Ben said. "That's what you would be!" He was leaning so far over the side of the bed by that time that he might near fell off and caught himself just in time, but that kind of quieted him down a little bit. He set back and said, "That's what I mean, Will. They're bound to hear about what happened last night, and we wont get in the

Infantry at all. One of them will let it slip and then . . ."

"No, they wont, Ben. If one of them says anything, I'll take him back and whomp him good and . . ."

"Now there you go again, Will! Didnt I just tell you? Besides that, it might be somebody else and they might have already told, because there was a whole barracks full of them that know it by now. There aint nothing that you can do and there aint nothing I can do. We'll just have to wait and see."

"Well, I dont think they will. I wouldnt worry about it none."

"Well, I just want you to know one thing. I aint blaming you for it because I was in it just as much as you was. But it does look like to me . . ." and he kind of turned his head away. "It does look like with me having bad eyes and all that they would take me, dont it? I mean, it does look like they wouldnt hold a little something like that against you, dont it, when you got bad eyes and things, just like they want in the Infantry . . ."

"Sho," I said. "I dont see how they could do that to you."

"Well, we'll just have to wait and see," he said.

"Well, I wouldnt worry about it none."

"I aint," he said. "I'll just wait and see," but he set there studying his fingernails and picking at a string hanging down from his sleeve, and I knowed he was going to worry because he was real stubborn that way when he got set on something, and was going to worry no matter what anybody said.

8

So we laid around in the barracks doing nothing for the next two days, and it was the hardest waiting I ever done in my life. Ben got worse and worse about it as time passed and I waited pretty hard myself, but I would forget and ease up every once in a while and get to talking to somebody or playing cards, because we was getting along fine with the others by then, and not even think about it until I turned around and saw Ben laying there on the bunk. But then I would quit and go lay down and wait myself, and it got to be pretty wearing. They kept posting assignments on the bulletin board outside the orderly room, and every once in a while somebody would come in and say, "There's another list up," and everybody would run out to look at it. Then sometimes they would come back and one of them would be grinning because he got in the Coast Guard or something, and there might be another one in the Air Force, and he'd whoop and holler, and then we would sit around some more, waiting for the lists.

And I waited as hard as I could, but sometimes I would get out my harp and play a few tunes on it, though I usually tried not to play nothing lively, only once in a while I forgot and did. I usually done "Mother Aint Dead, She's Only Sleeping," and those like that, which were quiet enough, only I would sometimes get to sparking it up some when I

warnt thinking; and the second afternoon this fellow come in whooping and hollering because his name had been posted on a list for the navy, and I played "Tennessee Shuffle Dance," for him while he done a right good buck dance, and I think I could have enjoyed it ifn it hadnt of been for Ben, laying there staring at the ceiling that way. But later we went down to see the list and Irvin's and Pete's names was on it for the Air Force and they banged each other on the back for a while, and then Ben began feeling some better about things because they still hadnt posted one for the Infantry, and there warnt many of us left. He looked at the list and give a sigh, so I give one back at him; and then we went back to the barracks and waited for another one to go up. There really warnt much sense in everybody going down except that somebody might think you couldnt read if you didnt, but we all went down because everybody was getting right anxious by that time. And then they posted two more Air Force lists, and it got to be right fun with everybody whooping and hollering and going on, just like a party or something.

So we hung around the barracks all that afternoon and in a little while it was nearly four o'clock and they still hadnt posted an Infantry list, and Ben began to perk up a good bit. He begun pacing around some and at four-thirty we went outside to watch them close down the office for the day; and then Ben looked at me and kind of shook his head, grinning a little bit. So I whopped him a good one on the back and he whopped at me too, and we went back inside where everybody was talking about where they were going. They hadnt knowed each other moren five days, some of them, but they got each other's addresses and said how they would write and all like that, and it was good being amongst them,

even though by that time me and Ben figgered we'd never see none of them no more because we would be in the Infantry.

And everybody was feeling mighty good by that time so when we fell out in front to go down to supper, just as we was getting lined up, I said, "Why dont you march us down, Ben?" and some of the others chimed in on it too.

But Ben turned red in the face and shook his head, and said, "Aw, we cant march yet."

"Sho we can if you march us," I said, and then Irvin said, "Go ahead, Ben," and even though he kept shaking his head sideways, we shoved him out front and got in line there waiting for him.

Lucky said, "Come on and tell us to do something," and Irvin said, "Yeah, you just call 'em and we'll follow 'em," and everybody else started calling out too because they was so full of spark and everything, and wanted to try some real marching this time because all we usually done was just line up and start walking.

So Ben finally give in to them and tried it. He snatched himself up real straight with his back in a curve and yelled out, "All right, Attention!" but it didnt come out so good— it only kind of squeaked out and didnt sound powerful the way it was supposed to, so he got all red in the face again and started to quit. But everybody kept on at him so finally he said, "All right then. Get ready . . . Attention!" and everybody was kind of *expecting* it this time and got in different kinds of stiff positions with their hands down by their sides, and it looked pretty good. The only one that didnt look much good was this fellow Pete up in the front line—what he done was spread his legs out about two feet apart and put his hands behind him and stand real stiff *that*

way, so he didnt look much like the others, and they had kind of an argument about it. Irvin told him that warnt no way to stand at attention, but Pete said he knowed it was because he had seen it before.

"No, that aint the way," Lucky said. "You stand real stiff and hold your hands down beside your side. Aint that right, Irvin?"

"Yeah, that's parade rest you're doing, Pete."

But Pete said, "Naw, what you're doing is parade rest. This is attention like this. You stand with your legs all spraddled out and put your hands behind you. That's the way to stand at attention." So then they argued about it a while longer until Pete got right mad about it before it was over. He said, "You remember that picture *Wake Island* when the Major come up to the fellow and said 'Attention' and the fellow looked around and give a jump and spraddled his legs out and put his hands behind him? You remember that?"

"No, I dont remember that, but I still dont see how you are going to march . . ."

"Well, I do," Pete said. "And if you dont, why dont you just keep quiet about it?"

But except for Peter trying to march spraddle-legged the way he done, everybody marched real good once we got to going. Ben give us a "Left face" and everybody turned to the left, and those that didnt got straightened out soon enough, and then he give us, "Forward march!" And then he begun calling out, "Keep in step. Keep in step," and everybody tried to do that, only there warnt much agreement on it and there got to be some shoving around until Ben started going, "Left. Right. Left. Right," and got everybody straightened out again.

Anyhow, Ben was something to watch after a little bit too. We went on up the street with him calling out "Left. Right," like that, and after a while it seemed that his voice kind of changed somehow so it sounded right powerful, and he didnt even look like himself no more. He was rared back and strutting real big with his knees going way up and his arms swinging and his head throwed back, and his voice getting louder all the time. Before we got down to the end of the barracks, he was going, "Hut, two, three, four. Left foot on one. Hut, two three, four," just like he was borned doing it.

And then he called out, "You had a good home and you left!" and Irvin come right back at him, yelling, "Right."

"You had a good wife and you left!"

"Right."

And then Ben went, "Hut, two, three, four!" and it sounded real snappy too. And then they done this other one that went, "Open the window and close the door!"

"Hut, two, three, four!"

"Hand me some whisky and hand me some more!"

"Hut, two, three, four!"

But then somebody went, "Get out of here and dont you ever again come back *any more!*" which kind of messed the whole thing up and got everybody on the wrong foot again and mighty near finished us off.

But Ben started calling out, "Left. Right," again until we got straightened back out and by the time we got to the mess hall, people was watching us from the other barracks with their heads poked out and waving, especially the ones that had just come in. We got to the corner and Ben give us a turn to the right which was the wrong direction, but nobody cared, so we just circled the block one time and come up on

the mess hall on the other side. Ben called out, "Detail, halt!" and then, "Fall out!" in just as loud and clear a voice as you ever heered so that you might wonder how somebody so little could yell so loud.

And Ben was right proud of it too. You could see it all over him. I come up to him after we stopped and said, "My goodness, Ben, where on earth did you ever learn to be such a marcher?" and he kind of shuffled around a little bit and turned his face away, and said, "There aint nothing to that. You can learn that anywhere."

"Not the way you done it," I said.

"Let's go and eat," he said.

So you can figger about how he felt when we finished eating and went back to the barracks and just happened to pass the bulletin board and seen our names on it. We was in the Air Force and was going to be shipped out with the others. Somebody had sneaked out there and put it up while we was eating. It seemed like a mighty low-down way to do, but there warnt a thing we could do about it. We went on back to the barracks and Ben climbed up in his bunk again and I didnt say nothing at all. I got out my harp and played on it a while, and even when I played "Saturday Night in Rocky Bottom," I didnt make it lively like I usually did, but let it drag real easy and quiet, like it didnt have no more spark to it than some hymn you sing at a funeral.

9

Anyhow, they shipped us out on the train the next morning and rode us all that day, and Ben was about as miserable as a man could get. He set there staring out the window at the fields, not like he was seeing them, but like he was just letting them pass in front of his eyes; and he rode that same way all the next day too, and I got right worried about him. I tried to perk him up by pointing out things, and when we finally stopped at this little depot and filed off, toting our bags with us, and we seen the planes circling over the town, I tried to get him interested in them too. Everybody was watching them and talking about them, calling them babies and all, and saying how this one could really zoom around and how this other one didnt have much speed but was really staunch and stuff like that, so I went over and said, "Look, Ben, that baby really climbs, dont it?" and made on over it a good bit like the others were doing. I throwed in a lot of Rogers and Wilcos and things, and then I seen this other one come over and said, "Look, Ben, that baby sho flies fast, dont it?"

But he only looked kind of disgusted and said, "Fast? That's a cub and it couldnt go no moren ninety miles an hour if it wanted to!"

And I said, "Ben, how on earth did you ever learn so much about planes?" and took on a good bit about that too,

but he just set there on his barracks bag and wouldnt even look at them no more.

Anyhow, we finally got on this truck and headed out for the field, and it was as pretty a town as I ever seen. We rode down along this street next to the water that is called the Gulf and everybody was laying around in bathing suits in the sun, and swimming and everything, and we had a barrel of fun all the way through. We rode along and yelled at all the girls, and everybody whistled and took on and made a lot of funny remarks like: "I'll take that one for Christmas," and "Buy that one for me," and all sorts of things that would tickle you, only it didnt tickle the girls much, only one of them who smiled back kind of sour and said, "Battle-weary recruits," which was right funny when you come to think of it as we hadn't been in no battle at all. So I got a big kick out of that one and laughed over it a good bit, but the rest of them didnt; they only kind of mumbled to theirselves and quit yelling at everybody.

Anyhow, when we got inside the field and stopped, there was planes all over the place, coming down low past the buildings, taking off and landing; and you could hear them down on the runway, roaring and blasting, the loudest things you ever heered, so I got to taking on about them again. I said, "Looker yonder, Ben, that baby's doing a chandell," which I had heered one of them say, and some stuff like that, and finally got him interested a little bit. And just as he was hopping down off the truck, a plane come roaring over the top of one of the buildings with its wheels down, so low that you could see the pilot's head sticking up in it, and I yelled out, "How'd you like to fly that thing, Ben? That would really be Roger, wouldnt it?" and he kind of nodded his head, watching it, and said, "Yeah," so that I

took on a good bit longer about it. I said it wouldnt be long before he was zooming all over the sky himself in one of them, saying Roger and Wilco and everything like that, and patted him on the back, and begun to feel right good thinking about it myself. I could just see Ben setting up there in one of them planes with his scrawny little head in one of them helmets, with caps and goggles and all, and I was just on the verge of saying something casual about how you couldnt fly no planes in the Infantry, when I heered this fellow calling out, "Will Stockdale. Which one of you is Will Stockdale?"

We was lined up by then and this fellow was standing out in front of us with a piece of paper in his hand with two or three others looking on. He called it out again and some of them looked at me, and I come back with: "That's me you calling when you call that name," which I thought up right off the bat like that.

"You Will Stockdale?"

Then I ripped off one I heered Pa tell one time that went: "That's what my Ma called me and I never knowed her to lie!" and everybody got a real big kick out of it and laughed and took on, only the fellow with the paper, he didnt; he only looked at me kind of sickly and said, "All right. All right. If you're Will Stockdale, you go with this fellow here. The rest of you stay lined up there."

Anyhow, I didnt know quite what was going on for a few seconds after that. I was standing there holding my bag and didnt move out of the line. But then the fellow started yelling at me, "Didnt you hear me? I said for you to go with this fellow here," and then this other fellow started coming over, motioning to me to come with him.

But Ben and them was ready to march off about that time,

so I shook my head at him and stayed in line. But then this fellow come on over to me, saying something I couldnt make out, so I tried to explain to him how I planned to go on with Ben and them. I said, "If it's all the same to you, I'll just go on with them, if you dont mind," and acted real polite about it, but he stood there jabbering at me and then grabbed onto my bag, and then this other one come over jabbering too, and the first thing I knowed, there was Ben and them marching away. So I turned to go with them, only this fellow was still holding my bag, and it looked like I was going to have to knock his head off to make him let go; but about that time I seen Ben waving at me as they was going off and remembered how he felt about things like that, so I didnt hit him or nothing, just give him a little jab in the ribs with my elbow so that he kind of gasped and turned blue in the face and staggered around a little bit. But he still held onto the bag somehow, and when I looked back around, Ben and them had got out of sight around a building somewhere, and I didnt even know which way they went.

So I didnt do nothing then. I just stood there and listened to them jabber for a while until one of them said, "Look, fellow, lets dont start nothing now. I tell you what you do. You tell the Captain about it. He told me you were to be assigned down there; it warnt my idea . . ."

So I said, "Well, where is he then and I'll tell him," and the fellow said, "You just go with Ringo here and he'll explain the whole thing to you. How about it now? No trouble, huh?" which was foolish as I warnt wanting no trouble with nobody and had been just as polite as I knowed how.

Anyhow, they kept talking about it and we stood around a bit while they kept pounding the fellow who had grabbed my bag on the back, trying to get the breath back into him,

and the one called Ringo said, "Comawn," or something like that, so I finally went along with him. And while we was walking along, he tried to tell me what it was all about and was right nice about it, but I found out soon enough he couldnt explain anything much; and I dont guess he talked more than a minute like that before I figgered out that the trouble with him was that he was a Yankee. He tried right hard, though, and I nodded my head up and down like I understood him, and didnt let on that I knowed what he was or anything, figgering when I got down to the barracks I could find somebody who could talk a little better. Only it warnt long after I got there that I found out the place was *full* of Yankees. The one called Ringo showed me to a cot I was supposed to use, and they were just coming in from drill at the time with their brogans and fatigues and dust all over them, chattering the way they do. So I set down on the edge of the bunk and rolled a cigarette and waited to ask somebody about the Captain. And they kept coming in, knocking the dust off and trying to talk, but not making much headway at it, so I kept looking for somebody I could make some sense out of. But all of them just seemed to squeak and jabber at one another, waving their arms around and kind of talking through their noses so it hurt your ears somehow, and there was a couple of them trying to cuss which was the most comical sounding thing I ever listened to—it was Holy this, or Holy that, or Jemminy something-or-other, and I dont guess I heered more than one good solid cuss word out of the whole thing. They was even worse than Bart, but they did try mighty hard, and I kind of admired the way they stuck at it, even though you couldnt make no sense out of most of it.

Anyhow, I still wanted to find the Captain so I sidled up

next to one or two of them and listened in, thinking it might help if I got closer, only it didnt; it only hurt your ears more; so I set around until I seen one that warnt jabbering so much and I went over to him and said, "Howdy" and he looked around and said, "Howrrr" which was about as close as he could get to "Howdy" but which sounded a lot better than the others anyhow, so I asked him. I said, "You by any chance know where I can find the Captain?"

And he said something like, "Urr besee surgen King furrz," which I found out meant: "You best see Sergeant King first."

So then I had to sit around until about three that afternoon to wait for Sergeant King. I laid around and blew on my harp and smoked and slept a while, but I finally got pretty tired of it and started getting anxious to get things straightened out. I started pacing around, feeling right ornery about things, and was going to tell them right out how I felt about things and get it over with and not have no more foolishness about it.

But time I seen Sergeant King, I knowed I couldnt do it that way because he was about the *saddest*-looking man I ever looked at. He had one of these long, thin faces something like a hound dog's and eyes something like a hound dog's too, and I felt kind of sorry for him time I looked at him. He come in and went into this little room up in the front of the barracks that he had by himself and when I come in, he was setting on his bunk with his face all droopy and everything, so that instead of telling him right off, I went at it real gentle and acted as polite as I could. I told him who I was and that I had just come in and so on, and he looked up and asked me what I wanted, and I told him I

wanted to see the Captain as I didnt plan to stay in this squadron but go up to the one that Ben and them was in, and felt like I ought to let them *know* about it.

But it affected him pretty bad just the same. He started mumbling to himself, rubbing his hands over his face, looking sadder than ever. He looked up at me and said, "I figgered it was you. Yessir, I should have knowed it time you walked in. They said they was sending you down here. And I should have knowed it would be somebody who thinks he can decide not to stay around no more, and will just *tell* the Captain about it. The fact is, they send every bum and idiot they can round up to my barracks and expect me to make human beings out of them—I never get anything but eight balls in this barracks and now they send me down one who says he's going to another squadron, and just *feels* like he ought to come by and tell us about it."

"Well, I'm mighty sorry to hear about all that," I said. "I wish there was something I could do about it."

"I know that helps a lot."

"Sho," I said. "Hit must be a mess having nothing but bums around and I would sholy like to help you out, only I figgered to be with Ben and them, you see. It aint nothing against *you*, you see. It's just that . . ."

And that's where I made my mistake too because his face beamed and he began shaking his head sideways like he just couldnt believe it, and then he busted in on me saying how decent it was of me and all like that, and how nice he thought I had acted, and took on that way for quite a while. And before it was over, I was hung for good. He seemed to appreciate it so much and everything; he patted me on the back and said how fine he thought it was I had decided to

stay around and all like that, so there warnt a thing I could say then without making him feel pretty bad about everything.

So we chatted a good while that way, saying good things to each other, and I told him how nice it was to meet somebody with good manners, who knowed how to be polite, and he said he felt the same and appreciated all I was doing; and after a little bit of that, he finally said, "Well, I guess you better go make up your bunk being as you decided to stay around a while."

And I said, "Sho, and if I was you, I just wouldnt worry about the barracks no more. I'll pitch right in and we'll get the place straightened out in no time," and then I reached out and popped him on the back and made out I was right glad I had decided to stay too, because I might as well have, being as I was stuck anyhow, even though I really didnt care too much about it at all, when you come right down to it.

10

Anyhow, I stayed around the place a few days because of Sergeant King. I went out and drilled some and begun to get along all right with the others, and they begun to talk some

better so I could understand them, but all that time, I hadnt seen Ben or them anywhere. And it was kind of a strain being around Yankees and not letting on I suspected it, so one day I took off and started hunting. I went all over the field two or three times and asked everybody I seen, through the PX and out to the firing range and all up and down the barracks, but I didnt see a one of them. I started out early one morning and didnt get back until nearly dark, and when I got back I was pretty wore out. So I went and laid down on the bunk to rest, but in a little bit Sergeant King come in and said, "I hear you dont like it here with us no more, Stockdale," which kind of surprised me as I didnt think he knowed I had left.

So I turned to him and said that warnt so, I liked it fine.

And he said, "Well, that's good because I was just scared you might not. Yessir, you had me worried today not showing up for drill. I hope you are feeling all right. You aint sick or nothing?"

"No," I said, "I was just laying down, all wore out mainly."

So he said that was mighty good, that he didnt want me to be sick because he had picked me out to go on KP and was scared I wouldnt be up to it. He said, "I thought of a lot of others, but it seemed like you were just the man for the job, being as you decided to stay with us."

"Well, I dont know nothing about it," I said. "But I'd sho be willing to try."

And he said, "Oh, they'll teach you all right. I got confidence in you, Stockdale. I'll bet you make one mighty good KP; in fact, I might even arrange for you to go tomorrow too so you can really learn it good."

Well, I didnt care too much about it, but I didnt let on—

he was happy and smiling again and everything. So I told him I didnt see how on earth he could ever figger that I didnt like his squadron, and who on earth would ever tell him a thing like that, and he listened, smiling, and said, "Well, we're mighty glad to have you too, Stockdale. Yessir, we're mighty glad to have you." And when he left the place, he was whistling to himself, so I guess it come off all right.

So anyhow that night I went on KP and there really warnt much to it that I didnt already know. I washed a good many dishes and then I helped clear up the tables and mop the floors, and along toward midnight they give me some potatoes to peel, and there's nothing I care for more than raw potatoes, so I et a good many of them; and later on they give me some carrots to take the heads off of, and that's another thing I'm pretty partial to, raw carrots, so I et a good many of them too, so by the time it was daylight, I was right full and didnt care for much breakfast at all, and only et a little moren one helping.

But I had been up all day and night by that time and was right tired, so I felt like sleeping some, but when I got back to the barracks, I met Sergeant King at the door and he wanted to know how I done and all, and I told him without bragging none; and then he said he had fixed it so I could get back on for the day shift too. I really didnt care nothing about it, but he stood there slapping me on the back and grinning and everything, so I went on back like he said.

And this time they let me work in the kitchen where they was having meat loaf and cabbage for dinner and those are things I always liked, so I didnt mind too much for a while, and kind of enjoyed nibbling here and there. I helped myself until I got tired of it, and then I went over to help this

fellow cut up some apples, and worked at that for a while, and et a good many, and was getting along all right until this cook came running over yelling, "Dont let that fellow get in them apples!" and made a lot of noise about it. He said, "Take him out back; I cant afford to have him in here no longer," so then I went out back and didnt get work in the kitchen no more.

So after that it got kind of tiresome because they put me on the garbage detail and I had to turn these cans upside down and wipe them out with newspapers, and then rinse them out with water and stuff like that; and keeping my head down in those cans that way kind of took my appetite away so I didnt eat much dinner at all. And later on that afternoon, when I started cleaning them out again, my stomach started hurting. It hurt all that afternoon and before it was over, I warnt liking KP so much, and was right glad when it was time to go, as I was right tired too. I was going to lay down and not even move until the next morning, the way I felt. It was about dark and I just dragged myself back to the barracks, so to speak.

But right after I had laid down, not even taking my shoes off, I felt somebody punching me and looked up and there was Sergeant King again. I was just dozing off at the time, and there he was grinning at me and a whole bunch of them standing around, so it was something like a dream you wake up to. I could hear Sergeant King talking and I blinked my eyes some trying to rouse, but finally give it up as I just didnt feel up to it at the time, no matter what he thought. So I finally just told him to go on and let me alone, I wanted to sleep a bit.

But then I heered him say something about wanting me

to go back on KP again, but I really didnt feel up to it at the time, and I finally just turned over and told him right flat that I didnt care a thing about it.

He turned around and grinned at the others and said, "You dont, huh?"

And I said, "No, I dont care a thing about it. You get somebody else this time."

But he just stood there shaking his head at me, and wouldnt listen to a word I was saying. So then I told him straight out how I felt about things. I said, "You leave me alone and I'll leave you alone."

"I'll leave you alone all right if you dont get up off that bunk."

And I said, "That's good then," and turned back over on my side and propped my pillow under my head and started to go back to sleep.

He wouldnt stop, there, though, like he ought to have. No, he stood there and started cussing and taking on and said what did I think I was, and said I warnt a decent air-man at all, and said, "They bring folks like you in and pay 'em more money than you could sell all the hoecakes you ever et for, and I have to watch out for you." He raved and ranted and took on real upset that way which kind of surprised me because he was so polite before.

But I didnt hold it against him none. I laid back and looked at him as long as I could keep my eyes open, and then I shook myself wide awake enough to explain to him how I felt. I said, "As far as that goes, if they dont want to pay me no money and dont want me here, they can sho send me back home if they want to because one thing I like is hoecakes anyhow, as far as that goes . . ."

84

But then he yelled out, "By God, don't you get smart with me!"

"What do you mean? I aint getting smart, and why does it worry you if I dont go on KP because they gonna get the dishes washed if I aint there just like they are if I am, and it dont make any difference to me whether they do or not, as far as that goes. And if they want to send me on back home, that's all right with me too. I never wanted no trouble about it."

And you should have heered him after that. He stood there with his face getting red and then he started carrying on so much, you wouldnt have thought it was the same man. He begun pointing his finger in my face and calling me cuss words that I hadnt even heered before. You couldnt sleep if you tried with him taking on that way, and I didnt see much sense in it. So I finally got up off the bunk and told him, "Now there aint no sense in making all that noise and taking on like that, Sergeant King. There aint any sense in it at all."

And he backed off, saying, "Stockdale, you take a swing at me and you wont ever hear the rest of it as long as you live."

But I warnt going to hit him if he would just shut up, but all the time he kept backing off and then he started that cussing again, so I stopped because I warnt going to *chase* him to hit him, and just so he left me alone was all I wanted, so I said, "You know you ought not to act like that. What makes you cuss me that way? I dont think you got any business acting that way."

"Look, Stockdale, I think it will be many a day before you ever learn enough about the Air Force to know what any-

body's business is. You better find out what you are talking about first."

So I said, "Well, that's all right. That's what I'll do. I'll go up and ask the Captain if you can cuss me that way and ifn he says you can, hit might be all right for a little while, but ifn he says you cant, me and you are going to tangle up together."

He stood there looking at me for a while, and started to say something, and stopped, and finally said, "Well, you ought to know you cant talk to a noncom that way."

"I aint talked no way. I talked just as nice as I know how. If I said anything that didnt sound nice, you tell me what it is and I wont say it any more."

So he talked around some more, but begun settling down real nice, and said, "Why dont you want to go on KP anyhow?"

"Because my stomach aches and I dont feel up to it."

So he looked at me some more and then turned around and looked at all the others and nodded his head and then grinned and said, "Why didnt you say so in the first place? If you're going on sick call, you dont have to go on KP. If you're going on sick call . . ."

"I warnt going on sick call," I said. "I just dont feel so good."

And he kind of grinned around at the others again, settling down some more, and then he chuckled and said, "He thought if you went on sick call, you had to go on KP anyhow." Then he laughed some and said, "You ever heard anything like that before?" and laughed some more like it was real funny and like he hadnt heered nothing more comical in his life, but none of the others did, they only looked at him; and then he chuckled some more and wiped the tears

86

out of his eyes and stopped and said right quick, "Well, you better be sure to get your name on the sick book in the morning then, understand?"

"Sho, I'll go on sick call if you want me to."

And then he kind of drawed himself up and yelled out, "And next time you go on sick call, you let me know. *I want to be notified in advance!*" And then he turned around real quick and stomped out and slammed the door, like he was pretty mad again.

He acted awful peculiar that way, and it was a surprise to everybody. They got out of his way and nobody said a thing until the door had slammed, and then they got to taking on like they didnt have good sense. They whooped and hollered like crazy people and one of them drawed himself up and yelled out, "I want to be notified in advance!" and they whooped and hollered some more. And then one of them come over and started slapping me on the back, and ifn he hadnt been such a fool, I wouldnt have liked it none. He yelled out, "I wouldnt have took nothing for it! Not nothing in the world!" and slapped me again on the back, but I just ignored him; I didnt want to sound mean or nothing, but when he slapped me again, I told him, "If your stomach hurt like mine, you wouldnt think it was so funny. I dont see nothing funny about a man having a stomach ache nohow."

Anyhow, they took on that way a good while, giggling and everything, and I got undressed and got in to bed, and didnt pay no more attention to them. I was wore out, and I guess I must have gone to sleep in a few minutes after that.

11

I had a good night's sleep that night but when I woke up the next morning, I still felt ornery somehow. I went and had breakfast and then went on sick call like Sergeant King wanted me to do and I got in the wrong line and got shot with the needles again, and then I got out of that line and got in the right one, and this time when I come up to the desk the fellow said, "Havent you already been on sick call?" and I said I had but that they had shot me with the needles again and what I had come for was a stomach ache, but he said, "Well, you cant go on sick call but once at a time. You better come back tomorrow." So I left because I didnt have no stomach ache anyhow by that time, and didnt care much, but I still felt *down* somehow, and just couldnt get out of it.

It warnt that I had nothing against Sergeant King neither because he was nice as he could be the next morning. He said how he didnt mean to talk to me like he did and all like that, and I've never been one to hold a little something like that against nobody, and I told him so. When I come back from sick call he got up off the bunk and asked how I felt and all like that, and then said, "One thing I dont like is for my boys to be sick. And if you dont like KP, I'll just see about finding another job for you."

I told him it warnt that, though. I said, "It's just that they

are always having potatoes and carrots and things and I get to eating too much . . ."

"Yeah, I heard," he said. "I was talking to the mess sergeant about it. In fact, he come to me personally about it, so we decided to find you another job. I been thinking about making you latrine orderly. Maybe even permanent latrine orderly, if you like it."

So I said that sounded all right to me, and he said, "Yeah, I think you'll like it a lot. I sure do, and I'll tell you one thing—it's something that has to be done *right*. I wouldnt put nobody in the latrine that I didnt have confidence in. One thing the Colonel always inspects is the latrine. That's the main thing he thinks about, and that's why I'm putting you in charge."

"Well, I'll sho try to do it," I said.

"I know you will, Stockdale," he said, smiling and patting me on the back. "And some day when you get good enough at that, I'll take you down and let you help me wash my car if you want to give it a try."

So we were on real good terms again and I done right good on the latrine. All the others in the barracks had gone to get classified, and I had the barracks pretty much to myself, so I just hung around and kept at it as it got right lonesome not having anybody around. I cleaned up things so they just shone and then got the bucket and the mop and cleaned the floor, and went over the sinks with paper, so you couldnt have got it much better. The second morning I cleaned it, Sergeant King said he never had seen nobody so good at it. He said I was borned to be in the latrine and he should have knowed it time he saw me. He kept on like that for a good while, and it made me feel pretty good too, so I done a pretty good job on it.

Anyhow, I stayed at latrine orderly about a week, and me and Sergeant King got along fine together. All the rest of them were still being classified at the time, and I asked him if I was going to get classified, but he said he doubted it. He said that as far as he was concerned, I had already found my classification, and that as long as I didnt mention it over in the room or nowhere, I probably wouldnt have to fool with it at all. "Yessir," he said. "Anybody that can clean a latrine the way you can ought not to do anything else," and he stood looking it over and his eyes just shone. He didnt look sad at all any more and I felt it was partly my doings too.

And one day he took me down to help wash his car, and I kind of appreciated that because that was one thing Sergeant King thought a good bit about. I mean he kept it in this garage off the base, and he kept about three locks on the door, and he had more things to wash it with than you would ever believe. He had all kinds of brushes and wax and rags and polish and stuff like that, and he showed me all about it, going around patting the fenders, and I dont guess nobody knowed much more about keeping a car than Sergeant King did. I mean a lot of folks just like to *drive* a car, but Sergeant King didnt care as much about that, I dont think, as he did *washing* it. But he really was good at it and I seen soon after we got there, he didnt really want me to wash none. Everytime I would mention helping him, he would act like he didnt hear me, or say something like, "I guess I had better do this part. You aint had much experience on this kind of paint job." So I didnt push it none. I finally just set on a bucket and watched him scrub, singing away and whistling to himself.

But he was mighty nice about letting me go down there

and I appreciated it. One time he got inside and showed me how he could let the windows up and down by just pressing a button, and then he showed me these little shades over the top of the windows that was supposed to keep the rain out. He got inside and run the windows up and said, "See, I can get air up here, even when it's raining," and all like that, only it was right hot and his face started turning red after a bit and sweat begun running down the side of it as he set there calling out, "See, I can breathe real good."

But his face kept getting redder so I thought the heat was going to get him and finally said, "Well, why dont you just get out and rest a while and then you can get back in and show me again later," but it was late by that time, and we headed back to the barracks. So I didnt really get to wash it none, only I didnt say nothing about it. He was so wore out and happy that it was something to me just seeing him peaceful again.

12

Anyhow, the next day for inspection I cleaned up everything real white, except the tops which warnt supposed to be white, and Sergeant King went pacing all round the place

examining bunks and getting wrinkles out of them and things like that, and telling everybody how to act, and just what the officers would do and everything. He worried a good bit about inspection like that, and he explained it to everybody again, and it happened just like he said it would too. The door opened and some Lieutenants and the Captain and the Colonel come in, and Sergeant King called out "Attention!" and everybody stood real stiff like they warnt breathing, and the Lieutenants peeped and sniffed around here and there, and the Captain went around looking over the men in their fresh uniforms, but the Colonel, *he* didnt waste no time at all—he only glanced at things and headed right past, coming for the latrine where I was standing at attention by myself, just like Sergeant King said he would do.

And he really was the most interested in latrines of any man you ever seen in your life. He was a nice old fellow too, gray-headed with a little mustache and looked like an uncle of mine, but I knowed it warnt as my uncle hadnt been drafted that I had heered—anyhow, he headed right back for the latrine and went in and looked around, nodding his head and smiling, and seemed mighty pleased with it. And I was myself when I seen the look on his face and seen Sergeant King kind of cutting his eyes around at him. But I didnt want to take all the credit for myself, so when he come back by me on the way out, I said, "Colonel, I hope you like how we fixed up the latrine for you."

And when he turned to me and said, "What?" I said, "The reason it is so clean was mainly because of Sergeant King there. He's the one behind it all; I just done the cleaning. He said he had never seen a man in his life care more about latrines than you do, and that's the reason . . ."

"Attention!" the Captain yelled out. "You're at attention there!" and he come bounding over with his face all red like he was going to jump all over me.

But I didnt pay much attention to him because I warnt talking to him nohow, and besides the Colonel held up his hand at the Captain to shut him up, and then he looked at me for a while and asked me to go over what I had said again. So I did, and this time I really laid it on good too. I told him how Sergeant King had told me to clean it up so good because he had never seen a man in his life that would come back and stick his head right down in the bowls the way *he* done, and I think the Colonel kind of appreciated it too, because he looked around and said, "And which one is Sergeant King?"

So I pointed him out, though Sergeant King was right embarrassed and kind of white in the face, and the Colonel went over to speak with him for a minute. I couldnt make out what he said, though, because the Captain begun talking to me, and seemed like he had got kind of interested in the latrine himself. He asked me if I had been doing all the cleaning by myself, and I told him, "Yessir, I been cleaning it for about two weeks now. I'm the permanent latrine orderly."

"You mean you havent even started *classification* yet? You've been here two weeks and havent even *started* . . . Oh, Sergeant King, step over here a minute, will you, when the Colonel finishes speaking with you."

So we all kind of gathered around, the Colonel and the Captain and the Lieutenants and Sergeant King and myself, and had a real nice chat about it. They wanted to know about what I had been doing and I told them about the latrine and how Sergeant King let me work there, and how

at first I was on KP for a while, and how nice Sergeant King had been to me, not making me bother with classification but letting me help wash his car and all; and we kept talking about it, only Sergeant King didnt say much but kept his head ducked down and kept blushing and acting modest and everything—anyhow, we talked and talked—and finally they got ready to leave, and the Captain said, "King, you come over and wait in the office. I want to talk to you a little while," and Sergeant King come to attention and said, "Yessir," so it all seemed to come off all right. And they was about the nicest bunch of officers I had ever seen and must have knowed me from somewhere too because just as they were leaving, the Captain looked at me and said, "You must be Stockdale."

And I said, "Yessir, that's right, but I dont recall meeting you . . ." but he didnt stay around no longer; he only turned to the Lieutenant and said, "That one's Stockdale," and the Lieutenant looked at me and said, "Oh, yeah," and I said, "Yessir, that's right, but I dont recall meeting . . ." but they were already headed out about that time.

Anyhow, you could never tell how Sergeant King would feel about things, as changeable as he was, and when he come back from talking with the Captain, he was most *wild*-looking in a way. He stood in his room and kept blinking his eyes and shaking his head like he didnt even know I was there. "You didnt have to do it," he finally said. "You really didnt have to do that."

"I know it," I said. "But I didnt seen no sense in me taking all the credit when it was your idea and all. You done a lot for me and I thought I could help out some and . . ."

But he kept shaking his head, and said, "Yes, but did you think that would be *helping* . . ." and then he stopped and

rubbed his hands over his face and said, "Yes, I guess you would. I'm not surprised at all. But look here now, you dont have to help me out no more, see? I get along all right here. I got four stripes and my own barracks and I dont really need no help. You've done enough for me already. Look, you help somebody else out for a while. Look, I know a loud-mouthed, low-down, four-striper over in the orderly room, why dont you help *him* out a little bit? Why . . . ?" But then he waved his hand like he didnt want to talk about it no more, and I said I would if I got the chance, but he waved his hand again and turned back around and said, "Look, Will, just forget everything else now. The main thing now is to get you *classified*. That's something we've *got* to do."

And then he seemed to get all upset about that too. He got to pacing up and down talking about it, seeming right anxious about it, and looking all worried again. So I tried to calm him down a bit; I said it probably didnt amount to much and that there really warnt that much to worry about because I liked the latrine fine and had just as soon stay right there as long as I was on the field.

But that seemed to upset him too. He said, "No, Will, no! You wouldnt want to spend the rest of your hitch here, would you? You want to get out and do something. Nosir, what we want to do is get you classified and shipped out of here, because the Captain said that if you didnt, you would stay right here and . . . Look, Will, if it's the last thing we ever do, I think we ought to get you classified. It's the *only* thing."

"Well, I was only thinking about the latrine and helping you out and . . ."

But he was the most upset I ever seen him. He said,

"Nosir! Nosir! Absolutely not! The Captain said . . ." and then he got all jumbled up with it all. He shouted "Nosir!" a few more times, and then, "They'll ship you a thousand miles away from here!" and a lot of other stuff like that, getting more and more upset. And finally he wore himself out and just laid down on the bunk and covered up his face with his arms, upset the way he was. So just as I was leaving, I said, "Well, if they *do* ship me a thousand miles away from here, I might manage to hitch a ride back every once in a while," but it didnt do no good. He only moaned, his face still covered up and didnt answer me at all.

13

So anyhow, that next day I got started with classification and there really warnt too much to it ifn Sergeant King hadnt of been so anxious the way he was. But he kept trying to tell me all the time just how to do and how I should act and all; he would get me off to the side and tell me how I must try hard because if I didnt, I might just have to stay there in his barracks all the rest of my life, and how he knowed I wouldnt like that and all, and he kept on that way until he made me feel kind of anxious too after a while. But I found

out soon enough there really warnt that much to it. It warnt nothing really but fitting a bunch of pegs in squares and things like that, and sitting in chairs that spin you around and all that kind of thing, so it was easy as pie, and wouldnt have been nothing ifn Sergeant King hadnt kept worrying at me all the time.

But I still done good on it all. I had one little argument with a fellow down at the radio place, and that didnt amount to nothing really—it didnt bother nobody but Sergeant King. What happened was, they set us at a table and give us a headset and a piece of paper and this fellow was standing up there talking about how we were supposed to mark down the dots and dits on a paper, but after they got started I couldnt hear no dots and dits at all over mine and told the fellow so. But then he got right unreasonable; he come bounding over saying, "Dont you know how to put a headset on? You got the thing on backward. How do you ever expect to hear anything with it that way?" And he said, real rough, "Look, put it on right. Dont you have good sense?" and some more stuff like that which I didnt appreciate too much. Then he got back up front and said this next one would be a trial run and in a minute everybody got to writing on their papers, but I didnt because they didnt sound like nothing but dots and dits to me, so I didnt do nothing but just set there, but then he come bounding back over saying, "You're supposed to mark them down! Cant you write?" which made me kind of ornery so I said, "I can write as good as the next man."

"Well, write them down then."

But he had made me kind of mad talking about writing, so I said, "How can I write down things like that? Those little dots and dits dont mean nothing to me."

"Look," he said. "It dont matter what they mean. All you're supposed to do is mark them in this column if they sound alike, and in that one if they dont. It dont matter a bit what they mean . . ."

And I said, "Well, as far as that goes, it dont make no difference to me neither, but they still dont sound like nothing but dots and dits . . ."

And he fumed and fussed some more with it, and said, "It dont make any difference what they sound like to you. *I* know what they mean and they dont sound that way to me; and they dont sound that way to the fellows that made them up, and they dont sound that way to the generals—so who are you to say they dont sound like anything but a lot of dots and dits."

And he kept on that way until I got right tired of it. I got up and told him he was probably right and that if him and all the generals said it didnt sound like that to them, then I just wouldnt bother with it and let them listen to it all day long if they wanted to, but then he looked at me and yelled, "Sit down!" which I didnt like too much.

"How's that?" I asked him.

"You sit down there and put those headsets back on. What do you want to cause trouble for anyhow?"

"I dont want no trouble."

And he said, "Well, sit down and take the test then. You do just what I said and that's all there is to it."

"Well, I can write just as good as the next man," I said.

And he said, "Well, go on and do it then," and didnt say it so rough this time, but more like he was asking, so I set back down and listened to the dots and dits and marked them down like he said. But it was like I told him in the first place, they just sounded like a bunch of dots and dits to

98

me, so I just marked them all down in the same column and left, because I really didnt care too much about it nohow.

So I didnt have no trouble with it really, only Sergeant King got all upset about it and took it mighty hard. But he agreed the fellow had acted pretty unreasonable; he said, "As a matter of fact, the most *un*reasonable thing he did was ever putting the headset on you so you could hear the things." But then he took on some more how I must try hard and all like that; he said, "The rest of them wont all be that hard, Will; and if you do like they tell you, I really think we can swing this thing. You hear what I say now? Are you listening to me now? Look, I've got copies of most of the tests and we can go over them here in the barracks before you ever take them, and that way, you ought to manage all right. But you've got to try, Will. You got to do just like they tell you."

So I did that and got along better on the rest of them, just to please Sergeant King more or less. We took some more and I done right good on them and Sergeant King was right proud of it too. And one of them I done good on, he said he bet nobody had ever done anything like that as long as the field had been there. That one made him the happiest of all, I think. What it was, was this puzzle made out of steel about as thin as your little finger, and the trick was to put it back together once the Corporal had took it apart, and they was going to time us to see how quick we got it done. The Corporal explained all about it before we started; he took it apart and put it back together and showed us, and said, "There aint but one way of doing it, so you have to use your heads," and all like that, and then they passed them out to us, one each, and one fellow got a stopwatch and the other one said, "All right now: Go," and the other one

mashed the watch, and everybody took to fitting them this way and that.

So I got to fitting mine too, but it didnt work out at first, so then I just reached down and got a right good grip on one of the pieces and straightened it out and slipped back inside the other one and tied them back up together, which was a right good way of doing it because I was the first one finished. So then I got up and give it to the fellow, ready to leave, but he looked kind of funny and turned it over in his hand, and looked at it some more, and said, "What did you do with this thing?"

"I put it back together like you told me," I said.

So he looked it over again and twisted it in his hand, and then he tried to pull it loose, only he couldnt make it as I had tied it up real good, and then he said, "You just wait over here for a minute until I get the Sergeant and see what to do about it." So he went over to the Sergeant and showed it to him and the Sergeant looked at it and tried to bend it and shook his head and said, "Which one done it?"

And the fellow pointed at me and the Sergeant come over and said, "What did you do to this thing?" and I told him the same as the other, and then he went at it some more but couldnt get it loose neither.

And then they started arguing about it, and the Corporal said, "Well, how would you mark him on that?"

Then the Sergeant looked at him and said, "You're supposed to be grading this. Cant you do a simple job like that?" and kept twisting it and pulling at it and getting red in the face.

And the other fellow said, "I'm supposed to mark it down if they put it back together or not and there aint supposed

to be but one way of doing it, and he sho didnt do it that way. How are you going to mark a thing like that?"

So then they called the Lieutenant over and by that time I was beginning to think I hadnt passed it. They all went off in the corner and talked about it some more, and then they got together on a work bench in the corner and got a pair of pliers and a hammer and the Lieutenant held on to it while the Sergeant started whamming away at it, and they mighty near got it loose that way, only he hit the Lieutenant's hand and the Lieutenant jumped up in the air and started cussing and slinging his hand around; and they took on that way for a while so I finally got tired of waiting and left. And it warnt until I got back and talked to Sergeant King that I found out I had passed it. And I was right glad I had when I seen how he felt about it. It made him the happiest I had ever seen him; he patted me on the back and said, "Yessir, Will, I think we are going to get you classified yet. It just goes to show what the Air Force has come down to."

So then we went back to his room and went over some of the other tests I had to take.

So I done right good on all of them and didnt have no trouble at all to speak of, only I run into this Major at one of the tests and nearly had some trouble with him, but I seen there was something the matter with him and stopped myself. But he was a real peculiar fellow and had a way of saying rough things at you; he wore these big thick glasses that made his eyes look about the size of a cow's, and when we come into this room, he was standing there with his hands folded behind his back, rocking back and forth on his feet, staring right at me, like he might have knowed me

from somewhere. So I looked back at him, and he kept standing there looking at me, and I thought maybe I had met him from somewhere, so I nodded and said, "Howdy," but all he done was just keep staring at me, and never opened his mouth.

So I couldnt figger him at first, and we stood around a minute and then he turned and went over to the Corporal at the desk and started talking to him, looking up at me every once in a while, and the Corporal nodded his head, and then the Major turned back around and looked at me again, and then went in this other room.

And in a little bit, they led us all in there where we set down at desks that had chairs on both sides of them, the desks lined up and down the wall, and then a bunch of officers come in and set on the other side of the desks, and then I looked up and seen this same Major just taking his chair right across from me. So I nodded and said, "Howdy," again, but he still didnt say nothing. He shuffled some papers around on his desk, not saying a word, and I waited until he had finished, and then he looked up at me, and started staring again like he did out in the hall. Then he asked me my name and I told him, and he wrote that down without even looking at the paper, staring at me all the time. And I guess he had the most peculiar eyes I ever seen. I said they was like a cow's but they warnt; they was gray and had black specks in them, and he kept them pointed right at me so I looked back at him, and it seemed we done that for a minute or so until he finally said, "Where you from, Stockdale?"

I told him Georgia, and he come back with: "That's not much of a state, is it?" which didnt sound very polite to me.

But I said, "Well, I dont live all over the state. I just live in one little place in it."

Then he kept staring and said, "That's where they have the tobacco roads and things, isnt it?"

"Maybe so, but not around my section," I said. "I never seen no tobacco planted in a road. Maybe you from some other part than me."

"No, I never been there," he said. Then he looked harder and said, "And I dont think I ever would go there. What do you think about that?"

He let it bust out and kind of leaned over the table at me, and I really didnt know what to make of him for a second. The way he kept making conversation I figgered he was trying to be friendly, but the things he said didnt make much sense, and I never had seen anybody stare like that before. So I didnt know what to make out of him. I said, "Well, I dont think nothing about it. Fact is, I aint ever thought about it before."

He said, "I dont think I would ever want to live in your rotten state. How about that?"

"Well, I guess you know where you want to live," I told him. "Besides that, things is getting right crowded around home anyhow. Some folks moved in not long ago about two miles down the road from us and land aint as cheap as it once was. So it really dont make no difference to me whether you live there or not, not that we wouldnt be mighty glad to have you . . ." I finally quit talking because he didnt seem to be listening nohow. He kept staring and by this time I was staring too.

"You mean you dont mind it when somebody says something bad about Georgia?"

"I aint heered nobody say nothing bad about Georgia."

"What do you think I been talking about?"

"Well, I aint thought too much about it," I told him. "Dont you know?"

So he went on that way for a while and then all of a sudden he just quit talking and kept looking at me, and kept looking back, and we done that for a few seconds, just setting there staring, until I could tell it was getting right hard on him. He started to say something and then stopped and looked harder and I looked hard right back, and in a little bit, he got his eyes all squenched up and mine begun to burn a little bit, and we done that a while, but I knowed he had to bat them sooner or later, and after a while his whole face was getting squenched up and then all of a sudden, he just stopped and cleared his throat and looked away altogether. He picked up the papers on the desk and wrote some more on them and then rubbed his hands over his face once or twice. Then he leaned back in his chair and I got ready to start staring again, but he didnt look at me this time. Instead, he started asking me about the most foolish bunch of questions I ever listened to. He asked about all kinds of things I had done when I was a child, and what kind of life I led, and all kinds of stuff like that, and then all of a sudden, he leaned over and said, "Why did you hate your mother?" which didnt have a thing to do with what he was talking about before.

"Sir?" I said.

"Long ago your mother beat you, didnt she?"

"Well, I dont remember . . ."

"Did you ever try to remember?"

"I dont know that I have."

"Dont you ever try to think of it at all?"

"No, I aint, but I will ifn you want me to. I dont think

it'll do much good, though, because she died when I was borned."

And that seemed to make him kind of mad; he looked at me and frowned real hard and said, "Well, why didnt you say so in the first place?" and snatched the paper around and wrote something down on it.

So I said, "I guess I should have all right," and said I just didnt think of it and so on, and then I figgered that maybe he was just leading up to it because he wanted to talk about his own mother, so I tried to give him a prod by saying, "Why? Did you hate your mother?"

"Certainly not," he said.

"Well, I wouldnt think so. Did she beat you or something?"

"Look here, now," he said. "You better watch yourself."

So I dropped it right quick. I said I just thought he might want to talk about her for a while, and tried to explain I didnt mean no harm, but he was still right upset about it and leaned over the table saying to me, "Well, I didnt say nothing about my mother, did I? I was talking about your mother. I didnt say one word about my mother."

"Well, I dont guess you did, and I'll sho talk about mine ifn you want me to, but it wont do much good like I said, because she died when I was borned . . . but now I heered Pa say one time . . ."

"Well, let's just skip it," he said.

"I can tell you what Pa said. He used to . . ."

"No. No," he said. "We'll talk about something else. What about your pa? Did he ever beat you?"

"Sho."

"Did he beat you hard?"

"Sho. Lord, I remember one time he took me out behind the pig pen and got one of them fence rails and leaned me over that fence, and Lord, I never got such a licking. Couldnt nobody beat like my pa could. I remember one time . . ."

But then he give a bounce and leaned over and stared in my face again and said, "You hated your *pa*, didnt you?" and kept his face poked right into mine.

And I couldnt think of a thing to say for a little bit. It looked like we was going to have to go through with all that staring again, and it seemed right silly to me, and I didnt want to hurt his feelings or nothing, but I told him then just as plain as I could how I felt. I said, "Sir, I dont hate my pa and I dont guess I hated my ma either, and if that's all you want to know, you can write down there on that air paper that I didnt hate neither one of them, and not my grandpa or my grandma either, because I like all my folks ceptn this one uncle I got that I aint too partial to because every time he comes out to the house, he's always wanting to rassle with our mule, and I just think he aint got very good sense because every time he comes out there he heads back for the barn and keeps the mule all wore out and tired, but there aint much harm in him neither that I can see cept him wanting to rassle with that mule, so I dont really hate . . ."

"All right," he said. "All right."

"So if you want to write that air down I'll be on my way and maybe you can find somebody else that hates their folks . . ."

"You just sit down," he said. "We arent half through yet."

"Well, now, I'm through with that much of it . . ."

"You what!" he said leaning over the table at me; but then he kind of stopped and set back again and rested a little bit

and rubbed his face, and when he looked back at me again, he looked altogether different. He was smiling as nice as he could like he had just seen me and we was old friends. And then he leaned over and said, kind of whispering it, "Will, what do you think about the girls?"

"How's that?"

"Girls," he said. "Girls. How do you like 'em?"

"What girls is that, sir?"

"Just girls. Just any girls."

"Well, I dont like just any girls. I know there is one old girl back home that aint got hair no longer than a hound dogs, and she's the meanest girl I ever did see. One time . . ."

"I dont mean that, quite. I mean girls in a different sense. When I say girls, I mean . . ." and he hedged around some more, and twisted and turned, and finally got way off the subject, and I never heered such talking as he did then. He got all wound up and wanted to know about girls in Georgia and I'd start to tell him and he'd say, "No, I dont mean that . . ." and then he'd be off again telling me about girls and what he meant when he said girls, and he got wound up so much it was just like I warnt there. He leaned back and put his head back and squenched up his face and talked and talked, and I listened for a while and glanced around and seen that most of the others had gone already, only he hadnt even noticed it. So I settled back and just let him go on and he kept talking about girls, only not about no particular girl but just about girls in general. So we chatted a good while about girls that way, and then I told him a joke I heered Pa tell one time, about Ike and Mike at the circus, and he was getting a right big kick out of it, leaned way across the table with his mouth open and his eyes all lit up,

until he finally noticed that the others had gone, and then he set back right quick and the grin come off his face and he broke in on me and said, "Yes. Yes. Well, I guess I better let you go now."

"Well, I aint told you the end of it yet . . ."

"No, that's all. That's not what I mean anyhow . . ."

So I got up and told him how much I enjoyed talking with him, and he said, "Yes. Yes," and I told him if he wanted to talk about girls some more that he ought to come over to the barracks because the boys over there was always talking about the girls and knowed a lot of good jokes theirselves, and he said, "Yes. Yes. Well, that's all. Yes. Thank you," and I told him that maybe if he went out and seen some girls every once in a while he wouldnt worry so much about them, but by that time he was picking up his papers and he got them all together and pushed his chair back and kept saying, "Yes. Yes," and finally said, "Well, I better go," and took off down the hall and out the door without even saying good-bye to me.

So I got through that part too all right, and Sergeant King was right proud of it. When I told him about how the Major had done and how peculiar he was and all like that, he patted me on the back and said, "Well, he was the main one I was worried about all right. And I think you done right good on it too, Will. The fact that you're still walking about in the open is proof enough of that for me. I think we might make it after all." And he seemed right happy about it. There warnt too much else to do, he said, and in a few more days I would be classified sure enough.

14

Anyhow, that next day was the one when I had to go to the pressure chamber, and Sergeant King stopped me on the way out and started telling me all about it again. He said, "You can get to be a gunner anyhow. I *know* you can. If you can just get through the pressure chamber, you can make it all right. And they cant prove you've got the bends or the sinus or nothing if you just keep your mouth shut. So you got to be *careful*, see? You wouldnt want to not be classified and have to stay here as a latrine orderly all the time, would you? So you watch it now."

And he kept on like that until all the others outside started yelling to get started, and then he let me go, and we marched down to this theatre where they was going to lecture us about the pressure chamber. And just as I was making myself comfortable to nod a little bit, I really got a surprise because down in front of me was little ole Ben's head sticking up over one of the seats, and there was Lucky next to him, and Irvin and Pete and all the rest of them! I couldnt even say anything for a minute, but then I yelled out, "Ben! Ben!" and he turned around and seen me and said, "It's Will, yall. It's Will!"

But about that time this Captain come nodding and smiling out on the stage, so I motioned them I would meet them outside. But then he said, "As you were," which meant to be

quiet, which we done, and started to talking and I thought he never would quit. He was a ground officer—you could tell because he wore this bashed-in hat and flying officers wear straight hats, and he kept saying Roger and Wilco and things like that, and flying officers just say "Yes" and "No" and he kept talking about airplanes all the time—and he was the happiest one to be standing out there talking of any I had ever seen. He told how they had planes that could fly thirty thousand feet up and how there warnt much oxygen up there and you would be dead in just a few minutes without your mask, and all about it; and then he told us about other airplanes that would go up to fifty thousand feet and kill you in just ten seconds, and make the blood boil right up inside your body, and all about that too; and then started telling us about all the other progress the Air Force is making, and I really got tired of it after a while.

But when it was over, I went outside to wait for Ben and them, and I mean it was good to see them all too. Ben and Irvin and Lucky and all of them come out and one of them hit me on the back and then I hit him on the back, and one of them shoved me, and I shoved him, and then one of them grabbed my hat and popped me on the back of the neck with it, and I stomped on his toes, and we had a real nice time of it. Then me and Ben went off to eat together and I seen that he warnt down on the Air Force no more, but was right excited about it, and I felt right good about everything. I told him how I was a permanent latrine orderly for a while, and Ben said, "Well, I'm going to be a gunner, I think. I believe that's the thing for me," and when he said *that,* I couldnt hardly believe it, it sounded so lucky. I had a mouthful of food and couldnt hardly swallow it even.

I said, "Me too, Ben. Aint that something, though. That's just what I'm going to be."

"Well, I be dogged," he said, grinning all over. "Maybe we can get together. I done passed everything now but the altitude chamber, and we get that this afternoon."

"Well, we do too," I said. "And I done passed everything too, and there aint going to be a thing to that pressure chamber because Sergeant King told me all about it, so I guess we might make it after all."

So we talked a good bit about it, and before it was over, I got about as anxious to be a gunner as Ben was. We ate and sat around for a while, and Ben got to talking about the Air Force and telling me all about it, and he made it sound so exciting and everything that you just couldnt wait to get in—and then all of a sudden, you would think, Well, I *am* in it, and it didnt seem like the same place somehow.

We started back and he begun telling me how it was almost as good as the Infantry in a lot of ways. He said, "You just think about it. If a man gets shot in a plane, he's got thirty thousand feet to fall, and the plane might blow up, or he might even die because of lack of oxygen, like the Captain was saying. There's a lot of things that can happen. And you know what they did in the last war, Will? They give out Air Medals for every five missions. That's how dangerous it was. And you know what you got after thirty missions, Will?"

"There just aint no telling," I said.

"You doggone well right there aint. You got the DFC, by gosh. And you deserve it too, Will. Just think of all the things that can happen. So you get a medal just like that, and you fly thirty missions, and what have you got—you got

at least four Air Medals and a DFC, and that's five medals in all, plus another one if you get shot or something, and some others for just *being* there. How about that?"

"It sounds mighty good," I said.

"Yeah," Ben said. "I believe you stand about as good a chance of getting them in the Air Force as any place. You take my great-grandfather that fought under Stonewall Jackson; he fought in I dont know how many battles, and he got shot four times and lost one leg and got his head bashed in, and didnt get but one dinky little old medal, Will. Why, that aint *beans* today. Why, today, you can get a medal by just not doing anything *wrong* . . . Yessir, Will, if we get to be gunners, there just aint no telling how many we can get."

So I took on about it a good bit, and we finally got up to the place where they had the pressure chamber, and me and Ben got to go in together. What they done was lead us into this little place that looks something like the front end of a train engine, and they talked to us some more about how we should do; and then they give us these masks and run us up to five thousand feet. But we didnt have no bends or nothing, so then they run us up to twenty thousand feet, and the fellow said over the interphone, "Now you're going to take off your masks and see how long it takes you to get dizzy. Each man watch the man next to you and when he looks like he has done it long enough, you make him put his mask back on."

So we done that a while too, and didnt have no trouble with that either, only Ben wanted to see if we couldnt keep ourn off longer than anybody else, and he got pretty white in the face before it was over. And I could feel myself getting right dizzy too and I looked at my fingernails and they

was getting blue-colored, and then I looked back at Ben, and he was setting there grinning sillier and sillier. And then it seemed like I heered him telling me to put my mask back on, and I tried to tell him to put his back on, and I said, "You put put put white," which didnt make no sense at all.

But he nodded and said, "Stonewall Air Medal and gunner."

I said, "That's put blue."

And he nodded his head and said, "Sho," and it seemed like we went on talking like that for the longest sort of time, and the next thing I knowed there was two fellows standing over us and somebody working on Ben's mask, saying, "Give him a hundred per cent oxygen. He'll come out of it in a minute."

Anyhow, we didnt have no trouble after that; they took us up to thirty-five thousand feet and we didnt have no aches, and then we come back down and Ben took off his mask with his hair sticking up every which way and lines on his face where the mask had been, and we got up ready to go. He said, "Well, I guess we done all right, Will. Now all we got to pass is the eye test and we're through for good."

But about that time, this fellow stuck his head in and said, "You two fellows come on in here. The Lieutenant will want to see you. Didnt you hear the lecture this morning?"

"Didnt we pass?" Ben said, his eyes getting wide.

"You mighty near passed *out*," the fellow said. Then he thought about it, and laughed and said, "Yeah, you mighty near passed *out*, that's what you did!" Then he chuckled a little more over it and told it a couple of more times, but Ben just stood there with his face kind of pale, and didnt smile, so the fellow didnt tell it no more; he said, "Well

come on. I'll see if the Lieutenant has anything to say to you about it."

So he took us down the hall and told us to sit outside while he went in to see the Lieutenant. Ben set there all hunched over with worry, and I was getting that way myself because it looked like we had failed for sure, but about that time I happened to glance in the office we were setting outside of and seen that the Lieutenant this fellow wanted us to talk to was a *nigger,* which was the most surprising thing because I hadnt seen many niggers since we left home. I turned to Ben and whispered, "Ben, they's a nigger in there!" but Ben only looked hard at me, and about that time the fellow come out and said that the Lieutenant would see us now.

So we went in, and I mean it was one of the most surprising things I ever seen. He was the *doggiest* nigger I bet there ever was, setting there at that desk in his Lieutenant's uniform. We come in and Ben he popped to and give him a big salute, but I was looking so hard, I guess I forgot all about it. And then the nigger said right out, "Didnt you fellows understand what the Captain said about what lack of oxygen will do for you at twenty thousand feet?" and didnt even *sound* like a nigger the way he talked. I dont guess I had ever seen anything like it before.

But Ben snapped out, "Yessir, it was a mistake, sir," and he said, "Well, be more careful in the future. You passed it all right. I just wanted to warn you." And then Ben popped him another big salute and twisted on his heel and started out the door, and then reached back and snatched me by the arm to get me going because I just *stood* there for a minute. I mean it's kind of a shock to a man to have a nigger set there and start talking and not even *sound* like a nigger, so when we got outside I wanted to go back in and talk with

him a little bit as I hadnt seen no niggers much lately, and never none like that, so I was right interested in how he *got* that way. I wanted to chat with him a bit because he sho seemed nice and was just as friendly as he could be, and there aint nobody any friendlier than a friendly nigger; so I wanted to go back in but Ben kept pulling at me by the arm, and then he lit into me all of a sudden. He said, "What's the matter with you. Didnt you see he was an officer?" which was a surprise to me too because I expected Ben would be right happy about having passed and not be mad about any-thing.

I said, "Sho, Ben, and I bet he is a mighty good one too, friendly that way and . . ."

But Ben busted in on me again, and lit into me about not standing at attention and not saluting and all, which I had just forgot about. So I tried to explain it to him; I said, "I didnt mean no offense by it. It was just that I hadnt seen a nigger in a long time and . . ."

"Dont call him a nigger," Ben said. "He's an officer! Didnt you see that?"

"Sho, Ben, I seen that; but I just didnt think about it, I guess, because he was colored and I hadnt seen no colored folks for a while and it made me kind of homesick and . . ."

But then Ben yelled out, "Quit saying *colored*. It dont make any difference about color. He's an officer, and being an officer, he's just as white as you and me, and you're sup-posed to stand at attention, and you're supposed to salute!" He got real upset about it, it looked like; and I couldnt make it out. His face got red, and when he talked, he waved his hands around and his eyes got big and all like that, and I couldnt figger it for a while. If I hadnt of knowed Ben were right smart in the ways of the Air Force, I would have

thought he didnt have good sense or something. He said all kinds of foolish things the more upset he got, but I acted like I didnt notice it. I didnt want to argue or nothing. But when he said that the fellow was just as white as I was when he was in a uniform, it didnt make much sense to me at all, so I said, "He was a nigger *really,* though, warnt he, Ben?"

"He was an officer!" Ben yelled.

"Yeah, that's what I mean, Ben. He was a *nigger* what got to be an *officer,*" which seemed to straighten the whole thing out.

But Ben shouted, "Well, that aint what *I* mean! What *I* mean is that when a man's in uniform, or any other place for that matter, but especially in a *uniform,* he aint black or white or yellow, or nothing else. You dont notice the color of a man in uniform!"

"You didnt really, Ben. Why, he sho looked to me . . ."

"No," Ben yelled. "Cant you understand anything?"

"You mean you couldn't tell he was a different color from us?"

"No!"

So I puzzled over it a bit but still I couldnt make no sense out of it; I said, "Dang it, Ben, I aint never heered anything to beat it! Time I seen him, I knowed he was a nigger."

He wouldnt talk about it no more, though; Ben had his own ideas and he was right firm about them, so I let him have his way. We walked on back down toward the barracks and I got him off on some other subjects, about what all we would do in gunnery and stuff like that, and he told me he warnt worried about the eye test any more, the way he was at first, because he had had them checked and they was better than he thought. Anyhow, he was in a right good humor again when we separated at the PX; we knowed where each

other lived by then so we could get together again right soon.

Anyhow, Sergeant King was real pleased with things when I got back; he had already heered about my passing the pressure chamber and he went around telling everybody about it and saying as how I wouldnt be there much longer and all like that, and when they tried to dampen him by saying something like, "He still hasnt passed the eye test, has he?" he would just laugh and say, "Why, Will can probably see right through any chart they got." Then he would go around humming to himself, and it made me feel right good too, seeing him happy that way.

So everybody got to feeling kind of sparky, and when we went out to march down to the mess hall, Sergeant King started to calling off one of the best cadences I ever heered; and I got to showing off a little bit and marched harder than I ever had. I snatched my knees up and down and strutted along and rared back like you never seen before, and when Sergeant King called out, "Count cadence, count!" I hauled off and bellowed so hard the ones in front of me had to kind of duck their heads. I prissed along that way and Sergeant King said, "That's mighty good, Stockdale, but it aint necessary to throw your knees up no higher than your neck," but I kept on with it; I was feeling right sparky myself.

And we had a right good time at supper too with everybody joking and going on. They started kidding me a lot too; and when this same nigger that me and Ben had talked to come in the mess hall, one of them tried to joke me about that. He had this band on his arm that said OD, which meant that he was Officer of the Day and had to eat in our mess hall, and he came in and got his tray and went to sit over at the table where the OD usually sits; and most of them were watching him, but I didnt pay no attention at

all. Anyhow, the fellow setting across from me leaned over and said, "Hey, Will, what would a Georgia boy think of a nigger officer?" trying to joke some more with me.

So I come back with: "I wouldnt think nothing of it because I aint ever seen one."

"Well, look right over there and you can see one right now," he said.

So I looked around and they was all waiting to see what I would say, but I looked right on past where the OD was setting, and then went back to eating again, shaking my head.

Then this fellow said, "Dont you see that one right over there?"

"No, I dont," I said.

"Setting over there at the table by hisself," this fellow said. "Look . . ."

So I looked around at the OD again and kind of strained my eyes and then I shook my head again. "I see the Lieutenant all right," I said. "But I dont see no nigger."

"What's the matter, you blind? You mean to sit there and say you dont see that nigger?"

So I looked real hard again like I was trying to make him out, and then I shook my head and said, "Nope, I dont think so. But course, I dont usually notice the color of things nohow." And then I went back to eating, only about that time I heered all these funny things from Sergeant King and looked up at him, and he looked right peculiar. He had a mouth full of food that he looked like he was getting choked on, and his eyes was bulging out and his face red, and he was trying to say something and swallow all at the same time. And finally he leaned over at me and said in a voice that didnt even sound like his, he said, "Will, you didn't see no nigger?"

118

"No."

"You see the Lieutenant?" His voice was mighty funny too, like he couldnt get the words out almost, and his face was so pale, you would think he was sick.

"I seen him," I said. "But I didnt notice no nigger."

"Will . . . ?"

"Yeah?"

"Will, do you think it might be that you're *color-blind,* or dont see so good, or something like that?"

"Well, I dont know about that," I said. "The only thing I know is what I just got through telling you. What's the matter, dont you feel good or something?"

But he never answered me. He just got up and took his tray and his face was the saddest-looking thing I ever seen in my life. He stood there and said, "It's possible. Yes, I guess it's possible, all right," and then he just turned away and started walking off real slow, like he didnt feel too good.

Then one of them said, "You know, I dont like him too much, but that's just going too far. I feel almost sorry for the old fellow."

"Yeah," I said. "I just hope it aint nothing serious. Maybe it's just something he et. I'll try to get a tonic or something down him when we get back to the barracks, and then he'll probably feel a whole lot better."

But they all just stared at me; I warnt too much worried myself, though. I figgered with a good tonic or something, he would be all right in no time.

15

Anyhow, Sergeant King was all right the next day, but then he had took to worrying about everything again. He said to me, "Will, you might not get to be a gunner being as you dont see too good, but that dont mean you're going to have to stay here in *my* barracks all the time. Now what we'll do, I'll talk some fellow from another barracks into putting in an official request for you, and then you can go see the Captain about moving, and maybe we can work it out that way, if there is a request and everything."

"You got it wrong," I said. "I see all right. I . . ."

But he was thinking so hard he didnt half hear; he said, "Well, just that you dont see too good then . . . I mean, you aint got a chance of passing that eye exam as far as I'm concerned, but maybe we can get you transferred to some place where you can maybe get ahead and . . ."

"I dont care nothing about getting ahead," I said. "If I dont get to be a gunner, I had just as soon stay here. But I'm still planning on being a gunner and . . ."

But he said, "Oh, no," right quick. He said, "No, you dont get the outlook, see? The thing is, there wouldnt be no room for *advancement* if you stayed here with me. And you've got to think of getting *ahead,* Will. And I mean I'm going to see that you get in another barracks if it's the last thing I ever do."

So for the next day or two, Sergeant King went around from barracks to barracks, but things didnt work out the way he had planned it, I guess, because didnt nobody ever make no official request for me, so he got all down in the dumps again.

Well, anyhow, all that week some of the boys in the barracks had been talking to me about going into town one night for a party, saying how they were going to show me how to shoot snooker. All week long they talked to me about playing snooker, and how it costs so much to play and all. I had thirty-four dollars, and they asked me about it nearly every day. They would come in and say, "Will, you still got that thirty-four dollars?"

And I'd say, "Yeah, but that seems a awful lot to pay to play a game. I . . ."

"Well, it's a real expensive game, Will," they'd say. "Fact is, it's a kind of gambling game. But we'll teach you all right. We sho will, as you say."

Anyhow, I hadnt paid too much attention to them; they were always taking on that way; but one day I happened to walk into Sergeant King's room and there was four or five of them in there talking, and Sergeant King looked like he felt a lot better all of a sudden. Just as I walked in, he was saying, "Well, I hate to do it, but I guess it's the only thing, like you say . . ." and sounded more like his old self again.

And one of them said, "Sure, drunk and AWOL—that will mean the guardhouse anyhow, and then . . ."

And then they seen me and one of them looked around and said, "Will, have you ever been drunk and AWOL?"

And I said not that I knowed of, and they all hee-hawed, and took on like they do kind of silly, and one of them said,

"There aint no bigger sport, Will. It's the most fun of anything."

Then Sergeant King said to me, "You ready to have that party, Will?" He was setting over on the bunk and looked like he felt a lot better.

"Sho," I said. "I didnt know you was going, though."

"Going? Man, I wouldnt miss it for anything in this world." Then he give a whoop and fell back on the bed laughing, and the rest of them joined in because everybody was feeling real merry, so I joined in a little bit myself. It was mighty good to see him all full of spark again.

"Yessir," Sergeant King said, setting up. "We're really going to have us a party. You ever drink, Will?"

"Well, just the stuff Pa used to make but I never . . ."

"We will," he said. "I'll see that everybody gets a pass, and I'll take my car. Yessir, I'll take my car and we'll go down the road and see the sights. How about that now?"

"Sounds good," one of them said.

"Sounds goodern good," Sergeant King said. "How about it, Will? You want to? We'll show you the town, in it and under it. Yessir."

"You still got that thirty-four dollars?" one of them asked me.

"Dont worry about money," Sergeant King said, getting up and walking around kind of excited. "By God, this is one time I'll supply the money myself."

"Well, we just thought we'd shoot a little snooker on the way, and that's a right expensive game, you know," this other fellow said. "And anyhow, there aint no sense in you trying to hog everything."

Then they all laughed and took on and banged me on the

back, and Sergeant King looked real happy about it. It was the first time he had looked peppy in about three days.

Well, they spent most of the day talking about it, everybody getting ready and telling me what all we was going to do, and how not to worry about nothing, that they would take care of me, and all like that. They said, "And dont worry about the Air Police neither if they say anything to you. If any of them bothers you, you just knock their teeth down their throat and that's all there is to it. Sergeant King can get you out of it if you get in any trouble."

Sergeant King hung around too, going to the windows and looking out at one or two little clouds that floated by and getting worried again because he didnt like to drive his car on muddy streets, but finally it cleared off and toward late evening there warnt a cloud nowhere, and he got to looking real happy again. And about dark, we got the passes that Sergeant King had arranged for and went down to the garage and got the car out. Me and a fellow by the name of Polettie and another one called P.J. who warnt as big as Ben and wore glasses too—we set in the back seat, and Sergeant King and another fellow by the name of Chris set in the front seat, and then we rode the five blocks into town at about ten miles an hour. It warnt too much of a ride because we had to sit right up on the edge of the seat because Sergeant King didnt like you to slouch back on the covers, and we had to hold our feet right still in one place so as not to stir up the dust in the bottom—but anyhow we drove the five blocks into town and about six blocks on the other side of it to park because there warnt so many cars out there and Sergeant King kept being worried about some drunk driver hitting it; and then we got out and started walking back to town. It really

123

didn't seem much worth it to me, but it made Sergeant King right happy having drove it, and it got enough dirt on it so he would have to wash it a lot more next week, so you couldnt gripe after all.

Anyhow, we walked back toward town with everybody getting real jolly and punching at each other and laughing and taking on. Sergeant King said, "We gonna rip and snort, aint we, Will? We gonna rip and snort."

And so I joined in with: "Like a hawngry hog, we is."

"Well, youse guys can rip and snort," Polettie said. "Myself, I want some whisky."

"We gonna have whisky too," Sergeant King said. "We gonna rip and snort some whisky too, aint we, Will?"

"That's rightern the preacher with the devil," I said.

"That's rightern rain on a tin roof," Sergeant King said. "Yessir, this here is a nice little town and it's got all the things a man could want, and the AP's are the finest bunch of fellows you ever seen. You can get drunk and rip and snort and kick the windows out and beat folks on the head with chairs, and they never say a word. You dont have a thing to worry about. This is your party, your farewell party . . ."

"Well, that's mighty decent . . ."

"It's nothing," he said. "We'll take care of you, boy. We'll see that you get back all right."

"And if we dont, the AP's will," Polettie said.

Sergeant King laughed and said, "Yessir, Will, you just let yourself go and have a good time."

So they laughed and joked and took on that way all down the street, and it was right merry being amongst them. Then Polettie stopped and said, "Right over yonder," and led the way over to where he said we could play some snooker. It warnt nothing but a pool hall, though, which kind of sur-

prised me; and snooker warnt nothing but just another way of shooting pool. But they was all excited and I didn't say nothing about it; they got down their cues and powdered them and chalked them up, everybody talking and jabbering, and then Polettie come over to show me how to shoot. He said, "You see those little pockets, Will? Well, all you got to do is take these here sticks and bump it against the ball here—we calls this the cue ball—and knock in one of them red balls in one of these holes here—we call them pockets. Then you get to shoot one of the other balls, see. A red ball counts a point and the other balls count whatever it says on the side. Then you shoot the rest of them in rotation, that means two, three, four and so on. See? Nothing to it, really. The only other thing is that it is usually kind of customary to put down a little bet. Now how much was it you said you had?"

"Thirty-four dollars," I said.

"Well, we'll just get everybody together and see how much of that we can cover. We'll let you cover all the bets at first because this is your first game, okay?"

So he went around and collected up twenty-seven dollars and they covered that much of my thirty-four. Then he laid it out on the table, and they said for me to break the balls because I was doing most of the betting, so I leaned over and broke them up and made me a red ball, and they took on about that for a good while. They clomped me on the back and said I was about the best they was and so on, and acted like real good sports about it, I thought. They said, "Okay, Will, you done made one point now. Now you get to shoot a numbered ball, any one you want . . ."

So I picked out the seven ball and sunk it, which gave me eight points, and they took on some more about it, only not

as much as the first time. So then I shot again and dropped another red ball, and then the seven again, and then another red one, and then the six, and went on like that for quite a while until all the red balls were gone. And then I started shooting them in rotation like they said, and I kind of got wrapped up in it, I guess, because it warnt until I was down to the last ball that I noticed that nobody had said anything for a while. So I looked around and seen they was sitting around just watching, not saying a word, some of them on tables and some of them in chairs around the place. Anyhow, I stopped then, feeling right bad about hogging all the shooting; I said, "Dont one of yall want to shoot that one? It dont seem right for just one person to do all the shooting all the time."

But none of them moved or said anything. Then Polettie put his cue back in the rack and said, "Naw, Will, you might as well go ahead and shoot that one too. We wouldnt want to keep you from learning how."

"That's all right," I said. "There really dont seem to be too much to it nohow. Dont yall want to rack them up for another one?"

But Polettie said, "There aint one of us that could afford the necessary dime," and they all started putting their cues back up, and it made me feel pretty bad. If I had of knowed they had bet all they had, I never would have bet with them in the first place. We went out of the place and I was right miserable thinking about it. I wished they was some way I could give it back without making them feel bad, but I couldnt think of no way at all. It aint ever right to act like a man aint willing to pay off his bets, and I know I wouldnt want to lose money to a man and have him try to give it back to me—you wouldnt even feel like a man no more.

But we wandered around for a while and everything got more dismal, so I decided to take a chance on it. I come out and said, "Well, now, I dont want yall to take no offense at it, but I'd be glad to lend you a dollar apiece if you need it for the night, if you just want to borrow some, being as we are going to have a party and everything."

They all stopped and looked at me, and I was scared I had said the wrong thing, only I didnt see no harm in *lending* them some; but then Sergeant King said, "That's mighty decent of you, Stockdale. Mighty decent," and took it pretty good. They all gathered around and I give them a dollar apiece; and then I told them, "I'll lend you another one later on ifn you happen to need it."

But Polettie said, "Another dollar? Why, I dont see how on earth we are going to spend all this one, Will," so I didnt bring it up no more, as I had gone pretty far in the first place.

Anyhow, we went down to this place they were talking about, and we drank some beer but it didnt seem like much of a party. The place got pretty crowded up with so many people that you couldnt move around hardly, with all kinds of different uniforms around, sailors and soldiers and so on, and there was so much smoke that the ceiling looked blue with it, and a big old juke organ blaring out so loud that you couldnt hardly talk to each other. We set in the booth and drank some more beer that I ordered, but nobody had much to say, only set there looking at the other people, and the thing got right dull for a party. We saw one right good fight, and we thought we was going to see another one because these two fellows started yelling pretty hard at each other; one of them kept saying, "Let me go. Let me go," to this little old fellow who warnt half holding him nohow, and kept

trying to jerk away from him to get at the other one, and the other one kept doing the same, until they finally got tired of holding them and let them go, but then they just got right close up to each other and poked their faces out and mumbled things at each other, and cussed a little bit; but by that time warnt nobody paying any attention to them and they quit, and the last I seen of them they was up at the bar drinking together.

I tried to liven it up some by telling them a joke but they just set there and fiddled with their glasses and looked at the beer, and sipped at it, and when I got through, didnt nobody even smile about it. Polettie and Sergeant King kept nagging at each other; Sergeant King said he wished he hadnt even of come, and Polettie said, "Well, this was your bright idea, not mine," and then Sergeant King mumbled something else, and nobody seemed like they was having any fun at all.

And it warnt until I mentioned that I might get some whisky that anybody took any notice at all. But Sergeant King said, "Yeah. Yeah, Will, that's a good idea. Why dont you do that?"

"Yeah," Chris said. "That way things might work out pretty good after all," and looked around smiling at everybody.

So I went out and got a couple of bottles and when I got back, they was talking hard and excited, and seemed a lot more lively already. We opened the bottles and Sergeant King said he would pour it and poured me a glass about full, and said, "Here you go, Will. You're the first. Drink all you can hold. We'll watch out for you, and if there's any trouble, you dont have a thing to worry about."

So I drunk it and they all watched, and then I poured

them each one too, and we got to drinking and everybody got to having a lot more fun. I ordered some more beer and we drunk that along with the other. Everybody got real lively and most polite, grabbing my glass and filling it up every time I finished, saying, "Drink up, Will. This is your farewell party, and I do mean farewell."

It didnt seem fair for me to drink most of the whisky that way, but they seemed to enjoy doing it, so I didnt say nothing about it. We got to talking about different kinds of drinks and little P.J. said something about how he liked wine, so I went out and got a couple of bottles of that and another bottle of whisky, and when I got back everybody got to having a big time. Sergeant King fixed a special drink for me; he poured some wine and whisky and beer all in a glass, and it didnt taste so good, but they kept saying, "How was it? How do you feel?" so I said, "It's mighty good," and then they started to fix me another one, and I drank that one too.

So we set and drank for quite a while and then Sergeant King tried to mix another drink for me, only this time he couldnt hit the glass and poured stuff all over the table; and then Chris took it and tried putting the glass on top of the bottle and then turning the bottle upside down, and then little P.J. tried it, and before it was over, they had spilled most of the bottle. So then Sergeant King said, "Cant yall think of nothing else for our guest to drink?" and we got to having a chat about drinking in general, and it was real interesting. Polettie tried to tell about some drink he knowed about, but you couldnt make much sense out of it because, even though he was talking right hard, there warnt no sound coming out; so I told them about a drink that this uncle of mine used to fix up with gin and whisky and beer and how

he always liked a little bit of kerosene in it for flavor, and they thought that sounded mighty good. So I went out and got a bucket and a little kerosene from a filling station, and mixed it all up together with the gin and everything, and they seemed to like it right well. They said my uncle sho knew how to fix a drink all right, and I told them that warnt nothing to some of them I've seen him fix, and after a while things got real sociable.

And then some fellow from the Infantry come in and one of them got to talking with Chris and pulled a chair up and drank a little with us. He said he was stationed somewhere around there and that the place he was stationed was about the worse place in the United States. Then Chris said it warnt no worse than the place where we was, he would bet, and the the other fellow heehawed, and said that where the Air Force was stationed, it warnt rough at all, and they talked a while about it.

Chris said, "Walter Winchell called it the dirtiest filthiest place in the United States," and the other fellow said that warnt nothing, that Walter Winchell said the same thing about his place.

Then P.J. leaned over and said, "Yeah, but yall dont have to pull all the details we do."

Then the Infantry fellow said, "Details? Dont make me laugh. That field there is just like heaven compared to where we are stationed."

And that seemed like a mighty nice thing to say, so I said, "Well, we sho appreciate you saying so."

And he said, "Yall dont have it rough at all. You have it mighty easy and just dont know it."

So I thanked him again because it looked like he was go-

ing out of his way to say nice things, but then Chris cut in saying, "What do you mean, we dont have it rough?"

"You got it easy. You got it easier than the Navy."

"That's mighty nice of you to say so," I said.

"Look, you dont know what rough is," Chris said. "You couldnt take a day of it where we are."

The fellow heehawed and said, "We got it rougher than any base in the country. They drill us fifteen miles a day."

"They drill us twenty," Chris said.

"You dont know what *hard* drilling is. You boys in the Air Force have got it made. In the Infantry, we *never* get it easy."

And then Chris said, "Well, look, if you think so much of the Infantry, why dont you just shove on off and quit drinking our whisky," which kind of surprised me, as it warnt the right thing to say at all.

But then the fellow reached over and got the bottle and hit Chris in the head with it, which surprised me too because he had been talking so nice just a few minutes before. So I stood up and tried to tell him he shouldnt do that but then he tried to hit me with the bottle too so I had to pop him one. And then I heered this bellow behind me and turned around to see Sergeant King standing up on the table with his hair all messed up and his eyes wild-looking, waving a bottle around and shouting like he had gone crazy or something. And then he give another yelp and went sailing through the air like he was flying and caught one fellow around the neck and they went over a table together, and then the whole place was fighting. I bopped one or two more, and set back down, and about that time little P.J. climbed up on the table looking wild too and tried to give

a bellow himself, only it come out kind of weak, and then he went sailing through the air at something or other but missed it and hit right on his stomach. And then I seen somebody pick him up and he went sailing back across the other way. I lit a cigarette and smoked it and watched Sergeant King running up and down the bar yelping at the top of his voice, and then I spotted Chris over rassling with some fellow on the other side. The only one that warnt in it was Polettie —he was setting there still thinking he was talking but without no sound coming out. Little P.J. went sailing past again; he hit and bounced and skidded, and then this one big fellow grabbed him on one arm and another grabbed him on the other arm, and they started arguing about who could knock him the furthiest. One of them said, "I'll bet you a dollar I can knock him further with my left hand than you can with your right," and the other fellow said, "It's a bet. Put up or shut up," and they started digging for their money, and then little P.J. started digging for his money too. He pulled out his dollar bill and waved it around and said, "I'll just take a dollar of that myself, put up or shut up!" and the fellow looked at him and said, "Look, boy, you're just throwing your money away—I'm left-*handed*," but little P.J. yelled out, "Look, by God, I bet them the way I see them. Put up or shut up!"

So they argued and took on for a while and I seen that the party was about over with everybody bopping everybody, so the next time little P.J. come sailing by I reached out and grabbed him, and then pulled Polettie out of the booth and took them outside; then went back in and found Chris under one of the tables and got him by the collar and pulled him out; and then had to go back in to get Sergeant King who was tied up around a table and couldnt get loose. Anyhow,

I finally got them all out and prodded them down the street, holding little P.J. by the collar because he kept kicking at everybody along the way, until we finally got to the car. But then little P.J. got down off my shoulder where I was having to tote him by that time, and decided to attack the car, and begun kicking at the fenders and making all kinds of noise. So I tried to stop him from that because I knowed how Sergeant King felt about his car. But it didnt seem to bother him—in fact, it seemed to make him right happy because he said now they would have to wash it again. I tried to talk them out of that, but they was all for it then, and went to piling in the car, and finally the only thing to do was just to get in with them and keep them down as best I could.

But they was the wildest bunch I ever seen by that time. We went driving through the town with them falling all over the place and making all sorts of rackets, and then Sergeant King drove off the road and went wobbling across the field with the car bucking this way and that, and come out on the beach and drove down there a while, from one side to the other. And about that time somebody said that was the best place they knew to wash a car, and Sergeant King said he thought so too, and so he headed it right out for the water. I said, "Sergeant King, I dont think I'd do that; you know what you said about salt water on a car and all . . ." but he never paid any attention; we hit the water going right fast so it splashed out in big sheets and slowed us down some, but then he got the car in second and drove along a bit that way, saying, "Listen to that power, boy. Listen to that power," and kept going that way until the water was about four feet deep. Then the car just sputtered and stopped there, and they opened the doors with water

pouring in from every side, and then they piled out yelling at each other, and then they took off their shirts and begun to wash. And in a little while, they seemed just as happy as they could be with Sergeant King whistling and singing and all the others joining in on it. Little P.J. was setting on the top and he was singing too, only every once in a while, he would get mad and start trying to kick everybody and fall off and splash around in the water. And they kept it up that way for I dont know how long until I got right tired of it and climbed in the back seat to get some rest, only I couldnt get comfortable there with it so wet and soggy; so I got out again and tried to talk them into going back, but they still wouldnt do it. They whooped and hollered and kept on washing and made quite a racket out of it; and in a little while this car come down the beach shining a spotlight this way and that, only he never thought to shine it out in the *water*, I guess, and little P.J. wanted to attack it too, so we had to hold him a while. But that didnt stop them neither; as soon as it had passed, they went right back to work again, singing and whistling to themselves.

So after a while I got right tired of it and said, "Aint yall about ready to go now? We got inspection in the morning and I got to get that latrine all fixed up, and yall got to get your stuff up too because the Colonel . . ."

But Sergeant King said, "Will, you go on off and leave us alone. You aint doing anything but spoiling everybody's fun."

"But you said that salt water warnt much good for your car nohow and . . ."

"There aint nothing better for it," Sergeant King said. "Good for the paint."

"Get off your shirt and wash," Chris said.

"Yeah," Sergeant King said. "If you dont want to help, go on back."

"I dont mind helping. It's just that we got to get back for inspection and I was going to fix up the latrine special this time because it might be my last time and . . ."

"You do that," Sergeant King said. "You go on back and fix up the latrine. We're going to wash this car and do it up good."

So there warnt any way of talking them out of it. I stood around a bit longer, and took off my shirt and washed for a while too, but I finally got tired of it. And then I tried to talk them into coming on again, but they wouldnt do it, so I finally just left them there. I slipped back across the beach after the car had passed with its spotlight going up and down, hearing them singing and splashing around even three blocks from the place, setting up the worst racket you ever heered in your life.

16

So I headed on back to the barracks and started work on the latrine right away. What I done, I took this long piece of wire I had and run it from seat to seat, because they are all

in a line, you know, and then I pulled it around to the back of each one so you couldnt see the wire, and then I run it over to the door so I could get a grip on it. I had to hitch it to each seat with tacks under the lid, so it took me quite a while to do it. I guess it was nearly two o'clock when I finished, and Sergeant King and them still warnt in. I figgered they would make it sooner or later though because Sergeant King warnt going to miss an inspection if he could help it, so I went on to bed. And I went to sleep in just a few minutes after that because that's what mixing a lot of drinks usually does to me. Makes me go to sleep in no time after I get in bed.

I didnt sleep long, though. I was up again before day and Sergeant King and them still hadnt showed up, and I begun to get a little worried about them. But I had the latrine to clean up, so I went ahead and got the mops and rags and soap and a bucket, and really got it to shining too. I never seen it look so nice. I was through with it before the rest of them got up, and then I closed the door because I didnt want them in there messing it up none. At first some of them wanted to use it anyhow, but I told them how I had cleaned it up and all; but some of them kept on about it, but after I explained to them what I would do if any of them went in there, they acted real nice about it and went over and used the one next door, all of them but this one fellow who didnt act so decent about it. He come up and kept jabbering about taking medicine of some kind, and I said, "Well, go over next door and take it if you want to," but he stood there saying, "I already took it, I took it last night. Look, I got to get in there. I mean it!" I tried to explain to him but he got to talking louder and louder about the place next door being all full, and then he got right blue in the face,

twisting around and whining and not making much sense at all, so I finally had to shove him away a little bit. And he even kept on it a while after that, but I didnt pay no attention to him, so finally he just started crying and left.

Anyhow, I begun to get right anxious about Sergeant King and them because I didnt want him to miss how I had fixed up things this time. We went to breakfast and come back and they still warnt there. I went ahead and straightened up their beds for them and made everything square, which was a good bit of work being as I had to keep my eye on the latrine all the time, and when they hadnt showed up after that, I got kind of anxious about it. And then some fellow looked out the window and said he seen the Colonel and the other officers next door, and said, "It wont be long now. They'll be here next. It's just too bad about King, I guess."

"Yeah, I was kind of hoping he would make it," I said. "The way I got everything fixed up for him."

And I no sooner said it than this fellow called out, "Here they come! Here they come!" And I looked around ready to come to attention, but then I seen it warnt the officers he meant—it was Sergeant King and Polettie and P.J. and Chris, just coming in through the door. They come dragging in, water still spurting out of their shoes every step they took, their clothes still wet and their hair hanging down in their eyes. Sergeant King had one sleeve torn off his shirt and one of his eyes black, and the rest of them looked about the same—I guess about the *worst*-looking bunch I ever seen in my life. They stopped in the middle of the barracks, water dripping in little puddles on the floor, looking around at all the bunks and things and then Sergeant King looked up all of a sudden and said, "Aint inspection over with yet? Aint . . ."

But about that time, the door opened and somebody called out, "Attention!" and the Colonel and the Captain and the Lieutenants come walking in. Sergeant King's head kind of snatched back and his eyes kind of popped, but then he snatched himself up to attention and stood there like the others done; and then the officers stopped right still too. They stood there right quiet, looking at Sergeant King and them, and for a few minutes it was so quiet that all you could hear was little drops of water dripping off their clothes and pattering on the floor.

Anyhow, I was standing there in the door with the wire around my foot and they come walking on back to where Sergeant King and them were standing, and I could see they was right disappointed in everything. Sergeant King and them stood real stiff, looking like tramps; and the Colonel first walked up to Sergeant King and looked him over, up and down while Sergeant King stood there so stiff he didnt even seem to be breathing, and the Colonel's face looked all droopy and everything. Then he looked up and down Chris and P.J. and Polettie, and then he went back to Sergeant King and started all over again. Then the other officers done the same, and then the Colonel looked at the Captain and the Captain looked at the Lieutenants, and none of them even said a word. And I was right glad then I had gone to all the trouble of fixing up that latrine, too. I figgered at least *that* warnt going to disappoint them.

And it didnt, neither. You ought to have seen their faces when I give that wire a snatch! The Colonel finally come walking on back, just like I knowed he would, everything still right quiet, and then he come poking his face in the door, and about that time I yelled out, *"Ten-shun!"* just as loud as I could! He warnt standing but about two feet off at

the time and I guess it kind of surprised him because he jumped back into one of the Lieutenants because it was such a surprise for him—anyhow, I yelled out that way and he jumped back and then I jerked up real straight and snatched my foot with the wire tied to it, and those seats popped up in the air just as nice as they could! They really *banged* too —they slammed up against the side of the wall so loud it sounded like the place was coming down.

So it really worked good that way, and finally the Colonel poked his head back in the door again because he had gone all the way outside when they started popping he was so surprised—he finally peeped back around at me and looked back in again, and me and those seats were standing just as straight as you could want, all of them right at attention! He just *stared* at them for a while. Then he looked at me for a minute, and he couldnt say a word he was so surprised. He stood there blinking his eyes for the longest sort of time.

But finally he got himself straightened out and nodded at me and said, "Yes, I remember you. I certainly do."

"Yessir," I said. "Sergeant King made me permanent latrine man."

"Oh, yes. Sergeant King did that . . ."

"Yessir," I said, and then I looked at Sergeant King and done the same thing I had done before. I knowed Sergeant King had asked me not to do him no more favors but the Colonel was right disappointed in him this time, so I told a flat lie. I said, "We thought you would like it. Me and him fixed it up for you." I looked at Sergeant King out of the corner of my eye and you should have seen his face. It was the whitest I ever seen. He was right embarrassed about it. "He showed me how," I said.

And then the Colonel looked at him and said, "Sergeant

King ought to tell us some of these things. In fact, I think Sergeant King had better come over to the Orderly Room again and explain a few more things to us!" He stood there looking Sergeant King up and down and then he shouted out, "Right now, Sergeant. Right this minute! And dont bother to get dressed up. I want to talk to you just the way you are—I'll enjoy what I'm going to do a lot more," and then he turned and headed out the door.

Sergeant King followed them out and for a few minutes didnt nobody move. They all come and looked at the latrine and stared at it like they hadnt never seen nothing like it before. And then Chris come over and stood there and looked at me with his eyes kind of blank, and started to say something; he opened his mouth but nothing come out, and then he kind of stumbled over and flopped down on his bed. I said, "I was getting worried yall warnt going to make it back," but none of them answered me; they just turned away, all of them but little P.J. who still hadnt come out of it, I guess. He hauled off and tried to kick at me but his foot got tangled up in the wire which tripped him up so that he hit flat on his back, which made the seats fly up and bang against the wall again, which kind of scared Chris because he come bounding up in the bed, looking wild-eyed this way and that, and then flopped back down again. So I picked little P.J. up and put him to bed; he was out like a light already.

Anyhow, I waited around for Sergeant King to get back and find out what happened with the Colonel, but they kept him over there for the longest sort of time. Some fellows who had passed by the Orderly Room came in and told everybody they still had him in there and that they had heered part of it. "He's explaining how he was at the picture show and some

sailors got to cussing the Air Force and when he told them they shouldnt talk like that, they jumped on him and beat him all night long. The only thing is, he cant remember what show he was supposed to be at."

"He told them *Forward March American Battalion!*" the other fellow said.

"Yeah, but when they asked him who was in it, he said Willie Hoppe, and he warnt in it at all."

"He's sticking to it, though," the other one said. "He said Willie Hoppe was dressed up like a Chinese."

"They warnt even Chinese. They were Japs in that picture."

"That's what the Colonel claims."

Anyhow, I finally begun worrying over what was keeping him so long and went over to the Orderly Room to find out. You couldnt hear nothing, though; the doors was closed and they had quieted down some. But all the clerks were setting around and while I was standing there, the First Sergeant come up to me and said, "Stockdale, I just wanted to tell you that you're going to gunnery school all right. I think you ought to tell Sergeant King about it when he gets out. I think it'll do him good."

"Well, I be dogged," I said. "I'm mighty glad to hear it."

"You aint the only one," the First Sergeant said; then he looked at the door to the office where they had Sergeant King and said, "I aint ever liked him too much, but anyhow you tell him when he gets back, will you? There's just so much a man can take, and I think it might help a little bit."

So I went back over to the barracks and waited until Sergeant King finally come back. We went up to his room and he was laying on the bunk with his hands over his eyes, holding his stripes in his other hand, and he didnt move when

we come in. He said, "Stockdale, I give up. Just go away, will you?"

"I got some good news," I said. "Guess what."

"No," he said. "I dont want to guess. I'll tell you what I'll do though. I'll stay right here and keep my eyes closed for thirty seconds, and anything else you can do to me, just go ahead. All I ask is that it is quick and silent."

"I just wanted to tell you I'm going to gunnery school. I just heered."

He took his hand away and looked at me a second, but then covered his face up again. "No," he said. "No, you're going to stay here forever and ever and ever. . . ."

"The First Sergeant just told me," I said.

"That's right," another fellow said. "I heered it too."

Sergeant King took his hand back off his face and looked around again. Then he set up real slow and looked at the others and said, "You mean he really is, and last night, all of it was for nothing? He was going *anyhow?*"

"It's a fact," the fellow said.

Sergeant King looked at me and shook his head; then he kind of smiled and shook his head some more and took a deep breath and said, "Well, no man can expect everything. I lost my stripes, but I can take it, I guess. I guess I can take it." He stood up then and started walking up and down, kind of talking to himself. "You just have to put up with certain things," he said. "There's no getting around it." Then he turned around to the others and said, "You think I'm bitter? Well, I'm not. Old King has a lot of juice in him yet. You think I'm going to let four little *stripes* ruin my life? Nosir, not old King! Nosir, I can *take* it, by God!" Then he turned to me and said, "So you're going to gunnery school. You're going to ship out far, far away and never come

back no more and I wont ever see you no more . . . you think I cant take it? With that, I can take *anything*!"

"I'll try to make it back every once in a while," I said.

"Yessir, with that I can take anything," he said. "Even my *car* . . . even . . ."

And then somebody yelled out, "Yeah, there it comes!" from the inside of the barracks and Sergeant King stopped and they yelled, "It's outside, King! They just brought it in!"

He looked outside the door. "They just brought *what* in?"

"Your car," they said. "They got it out there now. Look at that thing, will you? Hey, yall, *look* at that thing!" People were yelling to each other all over the place, running to the windows to get a look at it. It didnt look so good, neither. The seats was turned upside down and the back one was poking out through the rear window and all the other windows was broke, and it had weeds all over it and big dent in it, and it was the most peculiar-looking *color* I ever saw. It was hung on the back of a wrecker, parked in the front of the Orderly Room, and there was some AP's going inside. Sergeant King looked at it; then turned away from the window real quick and lit a cigarette and begun walking up and down, puffing, and rubbing his hands over his face. Then one fellow said, "You could tell them you was going to a drive-in movie and you seen some boat lights and thought that was the movie, and you just happened to . . ." but about that time, the First Sergeant stuck his head in the door again and motioned with his finger to Sergeant King, and Sergeant King took a deep breath and started out again.

Well, it warnt until I got back from dinner that I found out what had happened. I stopped by his room on the way

back to get my bags packed, and he was setting on the side of the bunk looking out the window. Some others was standing around but they quit when I come in, and turned and looked at me. I said, "Well, I guess I'll start getting packed now. I guess I'll see you around before I go so I can say goodbye, wont I?"

And then this fellow next to me said, "No use in that. He's going to gunnery school himself. He'll be right with you."

Well, it was the most surprising thing! I looked at Sergeant King and he just kept setting there staring out the window, and I couldnt get over it for a little bit. Me and Ben and Sergeant King would all be together. "It just goes to show you," I said, "that nothing bad ever happens, but what some good dont come out of it one way or the other," and Sergeant King, he agreed, I think. But he still didnt say nothing, just set there staring out the window for the longest sort of time.

17

Anyhow, we went to gunnery, and me and Ben both got to be privates-first-class which means you wear a stripe on your arm, only we didnt get to wear it long because of this

Captain that was in charge of our crew in transition. He was pilot of the plane and was always real particular, wanting you to wear neckties and such most of the time, which I didnt care nothing about. Anyhow, he stopped me and Ben up town one day and I didnt have my tie on, and we had a few words about that when I tried to explain to him how it was, which I found out later I warnt supposed to do—Ben said all I was supposed to do was stand there and say "No excuse, sir," which sounded like a kind of foolish way to talk to a man—so one thing led to another and we was recruits again; and besides that he changed us off his crew and put us in another crew. And Ben didnt like that too much because he said we was now on the *sorriest* crew on the base. He said everybody knowed it was the worst crew there, but I didnt much think so myself because I got along with them pretty good. They was real easygoing compared to the other one; it didnt make much difference with them whether you showed up for a mission or not. Lieutenant Bridges was the pilot and he was a Reserve and was the only one of the officers I knowed much at first because the planes was so monstrously big and because we flew in the back and they flew in the front so that we didnt see much of the others, and didnt know them usually when we did. But Lieutenant Bridges was a mighty easygoing fellow and didnt care much what you done; he went around most of the time with his eyes about half-opened and half-closed, just kind of dragging himself around like he was walking in his sleep, only he just seemed that way, I think; he warnt really asleep but probably only half drunk, even though it was kind of hard to tell the difference most of the time. And as far as I was concerned, I had ruther been on his crew than the first one because he was so easy to work for. If you took it in your

head you didnt want to go on a mission, he never would notice you warnt there nohow. I mean like this one fellow we had; he didnt fly hardly any and one day when he come out to the plane, Lieutenant Bridges didnt remember him and wouldnt let him fly with us until he went back to Operations and got a card showing he was supposed to be on our crew.

Anyhow, Sergeant King had got back to being a sergeant again by that time and had got himself a job in the Orderly Room, and me and Ben hung around a good bit, not doing much but going on practice missions, and Ben finally quit worrying about losing his stripe, and we had a right nice time. Ben still didnt like the crew much—he was mighty disappointed in them most of the time and said it was a good thing most of the officers warnt like them and all like that, but he liked flying a lot, so we went on most of the missions, not skipping them the way about half the crew did. And I didnt mind it much myself—it warnt much trouble because there warnt nothing to do in the back of the plane but sleep or play cards or set there and watch the country go under you. Finally I got a checkerboard and took that along, and me and Ben and this other fellow took turns playing each other, only the other fellow didnt play much because he was working on a model airplane that he took along with him. We never did get to know him too good, though, because he finally just quit coming altogether, and I guess he must have dropped off the crew because we didnt see him around nowhere for a long time.

Anyhow, there warnt much to it; when we was scheduled for a mission, me and Ben went and crawled in the back of the plane, and when it landed, we crawled back out, and never had anything to say to anybody except sometimes

when Lieutenant Bridges would call back to see if anybody else was around, and I was kind of enjoying it. And then one day I happened to meet the co-pilot up in Operations, which was a right peculiar thing because we was just standing there talking together and his voice sounded familiar and he said mine did too, and finally we found out we was on the same crew together. His name was Lieutenant Gardella and he seemed like a real nice fellow, and when I asked him what they done up in the front of the plane, he said, "Nothing much. What do yall do in the back?"

So I told him about the checkers and the cards that we played sometimes and he said that sounded mighty good to him and that he would come back and play with us sometimes, and I told him I would like to have him and that I wanted him to meet Ben besides. I asked him what his job was and he said, "Oh, I do different things. Mainly, I just let the wheels up and down and I stick to that pretty much as I dont care to take on anything more right now."

"How long you been letting them up and down?"

"A pretty good while," he said. "About six weeks now, ever since I got out of cadets. Next time we fly I'm going to let the flaps up and down too. Say, why dont you come up front and fly with us next time? Why dont you ask Bridges about it?"

"Well, that's mighty nice of you. I'd sho like to see you let them wheels up and down."

"Sure," he said. "I'll show you all about it."

He was a real obliging kind of fellow that way and you wouldnt think he was an officer at all just to look at him—he looked like he was only about thirteen years old and you would probably think he was a Boy Scout instead of an officer if you seen him, only he always had this big cigar in

his mouth and usually didnt seem real sober neither, which of course aint like most Boy Scouts as they usually seem right sober most of the time.

So I went out and finally found Lieutenant Bridges in the BOQ and he was laying down on his bunk and I had to stand around a while before I could tell whether he was asleep or awake with his eyes half open the way they always was, but finally he set up and looked at me, and I told him what I wanted. And he said, "Look here, you cant just go around flying here and there. Why dont you ask your own pilot?"

And I told him *he* was my pilot, and so he looked at me for a while and finally said, "Oh, yeah, I thought I had seen you around somewhere before. What did you say your name was now?"

So we talked for a while and he said I could ride up front with them on the next trip, and then I asked about Ben, and he said, "Ben who?" and I explained to him that Ben was another one of his gunners, and he said it was all right by him, that it didnt make no difference to him one way or the other.

But when I went back and told Ben about it, Ben said, "No, I'll stay in the back where I'm supposed to stay. I never seen officers care as little about things as this bunch does. I wish we had never got off the other crew myself."

So I told him I would ride in the back too, but he said, ' No, there aint any use in that. After all, the pilot is in charge of the plane and what he says goes, I guess, even if he dont seem to know what he is talking about half the time."

But they warnt all that bad, I didnt think, and I really enjoyed watching them work when I flew up front. We took off that day about dark and Lieutenant Bridges got the plane off the ground real good and Lieutenant Gardella let

148

the wheels up and done a right good job of it too, right smack up in the sides like he had been borned doing it; we went skimming out over the end of the runway and then Lieutenant Gardella got out a cigar and stuck it in his mouth and rared back and begun reading a magazine, while Lieutenant Bridges flew back over the field and then set it on the automatic, and then propped his feet up and leaned his seat back to go to sleep. I watched it all and it seemed like they done right good, and then I went back to talk with Lieutenant Kendall, the engineer, only he said he was sleepy and was getting his parachute under his head and sticking his feet out in the aisle trying to get comfortable. So I finally went back and set in the radio operator's seat, because he hadnt showed up, and watched Lieutenant Cover while he navigated; and he was the one I wished Ben could have seen because he was probably the hardest-working man I ever seen in my life. He was bounding all over the back of the plane navigating even before it was over the end of the runway, peeping down tubes and looking out the window and writing things down on maps that he had scattered all over the desk, then grabbing up one of them three watches that he had scattered around and checking the time, and writing that down, and then taking this camera-looking thing he had, and running back to the dome and pointing it out at the stars that was just coming out, and then running back to write that down too. He wrote so fast and so hard that twice the lead flew off the pencil and flipped across the plane and nearly hit me in the eye; and another time he snatched up a map that had this weight on it that sailed across the desk and caught me right beside the head; so I got up and moved down a ways after that as it did seem right dangerous being close to him working that hard but I

still watched him a good while and got a kick out of it.

Anyhow, I wished Ben could have seen it the way he went at things; he was so busy most of the time he wouldnt even talk to me. Most people that work hard usually like to talk about it a good bit, but when I asked him where he was navigating to, he snapped real quick, "Biloxi, Mississippi. Dont bother me, I'm busy," and wouldnt even look at me. After a little bit, we was well on the way and it was dark and the plane was quiet the way it gets at night, with only the sounds of the engines and no lights to speak of except little blue dials and the lamp that come down over Lieutenant Cover's head; but watching him work was enough to wear you out, so I got a little bit sleepy, and must have dozed off for a good while because when I woke up there was a big disturbance going on with people walking around and talking, and I didnt know what was going on.

Anyhow, I woke up and felt the plane going in these big circles, and then I looked over to the desk and there was Lieutenant Bridges standing holding one of the maps in his hand and looking at it, and Lieutenant Cover arguing with him, rattling papers around and trying to show him how he had figured this and that. Lieutenant Kendall was setting over there watching them with his chin propped up on his hands, and Lieutenant Gardella was up front flying the plane in these big circles, looking around every once in a while to see what was going on with the big cigar stuck out of his mouth; they was talking loud and everybody seemed real interested in it, and it seemed like Lieutenant Bridges knowed a lot about navigation himself even though he was the pilot. He was waving the map around saying, "I dont care what your figures show. I guess I can look out the window and *see*, cant I?"

"Well, you just check the figures for yourself," Lieutenant Cover said. "I got a fix about thirty minutes ago and that showed us right here, and thirty minutes later, we're supposed to be right *here*. You can check every figure down there. I figured that position by Dead Reckoning and I figured it thirty minutes from that fix, and I know it's right!"

But Lieutenant Bridges kept on shaking his head and saying, "Well, by God, I can *see*, cant I? I can look right out the window and *see*, cant I?"

So they talked a good bit about navigation that way and both took a lot of interest in it, it seemed like. Lieutenant Kendall was setting back there listening to the whole thing and he was right interested too, even though he was the engineer, and so I stepped back there and asked him what the discussion was all about. And he said, "What do you think it's about? They're lost again naturally. I been in this plane seven times and five of them we been lost. All I know is how much gas we got and if they want to know that, I'll be glad to tell them, but I aint going to worry about it any more. They can ditch the plane or jump out for all I care; the only thing I know is about how much gas we got."

Then Lieutenant Gardella called back and asked how much gas *did* we have, and Lieutenant Kendall said, "Tell him we can fly another forty minutes. I dont want to talk with him because every time we do, we get in an argument over where we are, and I'm tired of talking about it."

"I know what you mean," I said. "I dont like to argue about things neither, but it is good to see everybody taking such an interest in things; old Ben would be surprised to see it."

"Who is Ben?"

"He's one of the gunners," I said. "He rides in the back of the plane."

"Well," Lieutenant Kendall said. "I hope he knows how to use a parachute."

"Sho," I said. "I bet Ben knows about as much about parachutes as anybody you ever seen."

Anyhow we chatted a while and then I went back and listened to Lieutenant Bridges and Lieutenant Cover some more. Lieutenant Cover was still talking about his DR position where he said we ought to be; he turned to Lieutenant Bridges and said, "Well, who's been navigating, you or me? I got a fix no moren thirty minutes ago and that means our DR position is right here, about a hundred miles out over the Gulf of Mexico . . ."

And then Lieutenant Bridges come in with *his* side of the argument, saying, "Well, I might not have been navigating but I got eyes in my head, and I guess I can look out the window right now and see we're circling over a town half the size of New York; and according to this map or none I ever saw in my life, there aint a town at *all* in the middle of the Gulf of Mexico, much less one half the size of New York and . . ."

"Well, just look then," Lieutenant Cover said. "Dont argue with me, just look. You can check every figure I got here. My DR position puts us . . ."

"Well, I dont care anything about that," Lieutenant Bridges said. "All I want to know is what town we're circling over, and if you can tell me that, we can land this thing because we cant fly here all night long while you try to tell me there is a town of that size in the middle of the Gulf of Mexico!"

So they took on that way for a while, and then Lieutenant

Gardella and Lieutenant Kendall had a pretty good argument about one of the engines going out; so they discussed that a good while too until Lieutenant Kendall said, "Well, there's not any sense in arguing about it; I'm going to feather the thing." And after a little bit, they changed positions, and Lieutenant Bridges come up front and looked out and seen that one of the engines warnt working, and went back to see Lieutenant Kendall and they had a long talk over the engine being feathered too. Lieutenant Bridges said, "You are not supposed to go around feathering engines like that. I'm the one that's supposed to feather the engine. I'm the pilot, aint I?"

"Yeah, but you was too busy trying to navigate the plane when you're supposed to be up there flying it and . . ."

"All right," Lieutenant Bridges said, "but at least you could have *told* me we had lost an engine. I am the *pilot,* aint I?"

So they talked about that a good while too, and I set back and watched and listened, only I must have dozed off again because when I woke up, we was coming in for a landing. We hit and bounced once pretty hard so that I got throwed halfway across the plane, and then bounced again so that it throwed me back where I started from, but then I grabbed on and didnt get throwed no more on the rest of the bounces. We taxied up the runway with the wheels squeaking and finally stopped and started getting out, but nobody was talking much by then except Lieutenant Gardella—he kept telling Lieutenant Bridges that he thought the *third* bounce was the smoothest of all, but Lieutenant Bridges didnt seem to care about talking about it none, and I noticed in a minute that none of the others did either.

Anyhow, we got out and they had this truck waiting for

153

us and we got on that, and nobody was discussing nothing by this time, and I was right sorry for that because I wanted Ben to hear them because they was right interesting to listen to. But everybody just set there and then Lieutenant Cover come out with all his maps and everything folded up, and he got in and didnt say a word to nobody either. The truck finally started up and we headed across the ramp with everybody real quiet until finally Lieutenant Bridges leaned over and tapped Lieutenant Cover on the shoulder and said, "Look, Cover, I dont mean to run this thing into the ground, but I would appreciate it if you would try to find out where this place is. I mean if it is in the middle of the Gulf of Mexico, we've damn well discovered something."

And then Lieutenant Cover said, "Well, the way you fly, it's a wonder we didnt end up there anyhow."

So we drove up and got off and everybody stood around for a while hemming and hawing, and Lieutenant Bridges went over and asked Lieutenant Cover again if he had figured out where we was, and Lieutenant Cover said, "I thought you was the one who knew so much about it. If you want to find out, why dont you ask the driver?"

But then Lieutenant Bridges said, "Ask the driver? You expect me to land a plane and then go over and ask a truck driver where I landed it?" and got right stubborn about it. But then he turned to me and said, "Hey, what was your name now?"

"Stockdale," I said.

"Look, Stockdale," he said. "How about scouting around here somewhere and see if you cant find out what place this is, will you? Be kind of casual about it, you know."

So I went down the way and asked a fellow and he told me Houston, Texas, and I come back and told Lieutenant

Bridges and he seemed to feel much better about things then. "Well, Houston aint such a bad town after all," he said. "By gosh, Cover, you're getting better every day. You didnt miss the field but about four hundred and fifty miles this time."

Then Lieutenant Cover said, "Well, what I figgered was that you would bounce the rest of the way—it looked like it from the way we landed . . ."

And then Lieutenant Bridges had something to say to that, and after a while they begun squabbling a little bit, which I didnt like to hear. Me and Ben stood around waiting while they went at it and Ben said to me, "I never heered a bunch of officers argue so much in my life!"

"Yeah, Ben, they do now, but you ought to have been in the front of that plane and seen the way they worked. That was something else. If you could have seen that, you would have thought a lot more of them. Why, I'll bet they are about as good a crew as you can find, when they're sober like that."

"Which aint often," Ben said.

Anyhow, I hated for Ben to hear the squabbling and kept on talking to him until they had finished up with it because he got so disgusted about things like that. But they was finally finished; all of them heading across the ramp except Lieutenant Cover who had lost the argument because they had all jumped on him together before it was over—he was getting all his charts and stuff up and mumbling to himself. And I felt right sorry for him the way he had lost out on the argument and everything; I went over to him and said, "Well, I wouldnt worry about it none. I dont see how it amounts to too much. I had just as soon land at this field as

any other one, and we aint going to be here but one day nohow . . ."

But he was right down on things and turned around and looked at me like he was almost mad with me, and said, "Look, do you want to check my figures? Do you want to check them and see for yourself? I got them all right here!"

"Well, I dont know nothing about it," I said. "If you say they're right, I guess they is."

"I can show you my DR position," he said. "It shows us right out in the Gulf."

"Well, I wouldnt know about that," I said. "If you say your DR position is out in the Gulf, I reckon that's where it is all right. How long do you expect it to be out there?"

But he was pretty much down on things; he turned away and stomped off without even answering me—nothing you could say would make him feel any better.

18

But after supper, it looked like things might work out some better. Me and Ben went over to see Lieutenant Bridges and them and they were all setting around the room and had a couple of bottles on the table and were getting along fine

together. When we come in, Lieutenant Bridges was saying that he didnt care if he was in Houston, he thought Lieutenant Cover was a good navigator, and Lieutenant Cover said he didnt care if Lieutenant Bridges did almost bounce the plane off the runway every time he landed it, that he were right satisfied with somebody that just knew how to get the thing on the ground. They kept passing the bottle around and then they noticed me and Ben there and offered us some but Ben didnt drink and I didnt care for none either; so we stood around until they started to squabbling some more again, and then me and Ben left and went in town to a picture show. Ben was right disgusted with them all again because he said that warnt no way for officers to act, and I said, "How's that, Ben?" and he said, "Drinking and arguing and taking on like that. Officers dont do that. Besides, if they do have to act like that, they ought not to do it around us because we are enlisted men. I dont know what makes that bunch do that way. They dont act like officers at all."

Anyhow, after the show we went back by their room again to find out what time they were taking off the next day, only we didnt find out much because they was still at it. They was arguing pretty hot this time and had finished up a couple of bottles that lay on the table and had opened up another one, and I dont reckon they even knowed me and Ben was there. Lieutenant Bridges was talking to Lieutenant Kendall about the engine going out and wanting to know why. He said, "You're the engineer, aint you? You're supposed to know those things."

"Was I flying the plane? Did I do anything to make it go out?"

"That dont matter, Ken. You're supposed to fix it."

"I never wanted to be a flight engineer nohow," Lieutenant Kendall said. "What I wanted to do was run an Officer's Club."

So then Lieutenant Cover wanted to drink to all the men that run the Officer's Club, but Lieutenant Gardella wouldnt because he said they all wore mustaches and that he knowed one that had a mustache two inches long; but then Lieutenant Cover said he knowed one that didnt have a mustache and so Lieutenant Gardella said he would drink to that one all right. "Did you ever see the one at Baker Field?" Lieutenant Cover said. "That man had the biggest ears of any man I ever seen. You remember him? He couldnt get them under the earphones. He would have to tuck them in. He was a Major."

"Let's drink to him too."

"I remember one time," Lieutenant Cover said, "he had these real *small* earphones, and he couldnt get all of his ear under them, and he worked and worked . . ."

"Well, let's drink to him too," Lieutenant Gardella said. "You all the time talking. Dont you ever want to drink to anybody? Why dont we stop all this talking about people and do some drinking to them?"

So they all begun arguing some more, so me and Ben never found out a thing, and finally just left there and went back to our place and figgered we would get out there early in the morning and meet them there. Well, we got there about seven o'clock and set around about two hours before any of them showed up, and once I looked at them, I kind of wished they hadnt showed up at all. Lieutenant Bridges' hair was sticking straight up on his head and what you could see of his eyes was all red, and he had his parachute on backward so that it hung down in front of his stomach and

mighty near tripped him every step he took. He come wad-dling along that way, giggling silly about something that Lieutenant Cover had said, and we went up to speak to them and none of them even knowed us at first. Then the others come along and they looked just about the same as Lieutenant Bridges; they had been up all night long and they acted the silliest of any bunch of grown men I ever saw in my life. Ben wouldnt even look at them he was so disgusted. There was a truck there waiting for us, and when we got up, Lieutenant Bridges stood up on the back of it and held his nose like a kid ready to jump in swimming and hollered, "Here's the way I'm going to bail out!" and went jumping way up in the air and falling on his back hard enough to break it, it seemed like; and then Lieutenant Cover stood up and he had his suit on backward too, and he yelled out, "Well, *here's* the way *I'm* going to bail out!" and then he went sailing through the air too and hit flat on his back on the cement too; and they laid there with their backs nearly broke, kicking their feet around in the air and laughing their silly heads off.

It looked like we never would get started, and from the looks of them I didnt much care if we didnt. I looked at Ben and his face was all white and his eyes popping out, so I guess he felt the same as me. The driver of the truck had his head poked out the window looking at them because he couldnt start with them laying all over the runway, and there didnt seem to be no way to get them all on at the same time. I mean Ben didnt like it too much neither. They warnt the best crew on earth sober, and *drunk,* I dont guess they's ever been another one like them. I looked at Lieutenant Gardella, though, and thought it might work out all right because he was the only one that had his parachute on

right; he was sitting there pretty quiet holding a lunch pail in his lap, and was just watching the others and not saying a word about it one way or the other. When they come climbing back up in the truck, grunting and puffing, he just stared at them and held his lips tight together and shook his head sideways, disgusted. And when they climbed up on the side and held their noses and went sailing out in the air again, Lieutenant Gardella didnt say a word; he just reached back and patted his chute on his back like he was making sure it was on in the right place. He warnt taking on and giggling like them at all, so I turned to Ben and said, "Well, maybe Lieutenant Gardella can do it all right. He lets them wheels up real good, I know," and Ben kind of nodded his head, though he was still right pale; but about that time Lieutenant Gardella stood up and looked around at us and said right quiet and serious, "I thought they had better sense than that. Now here's the way you really ought to bail out," and dived off head first the way you are supposed to. He hit on his face and it knocked him out for a while and we finally had to get down and haul him back on the truck.

Lieutenant Cover was the only one that hadnt jumped off and was the only one quiet, but he had his chute on backward too, and couldnt fly the plane nohow. And I mean by that time, I was getting right worried with them.

Anyhow, we finally got them all on the truck and got out to the plane, and Ben's face was about as white as I ever seen it. I never seen him so disgusted. I tried to get him not to notice what was going on and everything by walking around real straight and saying, "Sir," to everybody, but it didnt help none. He just set there with his face white and said, "They never *can* fly this plane, Will, in the shape

they're in, but we'll have to go along with them. We'll just *have* to go."

Then Lieutenant Bridges come up to me while we were standing around and said, "Where did yall go last night?" and I popped up real straight and said, "No excuse, sir," even though it didnt make no sense, but I said it loud enough for Ben to hear me; but then Lieutenant Bridges said, "Well, that's a silly place to go. What made you think of going there?" which didnt make no sense neither, but I said again, "No excuse, sir," and saluted, but I could see Ben out of the corner of my eye shaking his head sideways. So I give up and said, "We went to town. Where did yall go?"

And he said, "No excuse, sir," and went to giggling again; and in a minute I heered him around the other side of the plane saying to somebody, "Ask me where I went last night," and they asked him, and he said, "No excuse, sir," and commenced to giggle again.

Anyhow, there was two mechanics on top of the plane when we got there and they had the cowling off the number two engine with a little ladder running up to it, and finally one of them climbed down and come over to Lieutenant Bridges and said, "Number two engine is out, sir, and there's a mag drop on number three. It's in no condition to fly at this time."

And Lieutenant Bridges said, "What do you mean, it's in no condition to fly!"

"Well, it just aint," the fellow said. "It's in bad shape and . . ."

"What's the matter with you?" Lieutenant Bridges yelled at him. "Dont you have any guts?"

"Well, it aint a matter of that, sir," the fellow said, "because I'm stationed here and dont fly nohow, so it aint a matter of guts with me, I just think . . ."

"I used to fly planes that didnt have but one little bitty engine," Lieutenant Bridges said. "And here I've got more engines than I can even *count*—I dont even know how many engines I *do* have on this plane, and you come up here telling me about one little ole bitty engine . . ."

"Well, I . . ."

"Who took those cowlings off anyhow? Put them back on," Lieutenant Bridges said. "What's this Air Force coming to anyhow."

So they took on that way a while, and Ben got to worrying more and more about it. He said he didnt think they could fly the plane at all, so I said, "Well, Ben, if you want me to, I'll clomp them, and maybe when they come to . . ."

But he shook his head and said, "You cant do that, Will. They're officers and if you clomped them, that would be the worse thing you can do. The only thing we could do is try to talk them out of it, and we aint even supposed to do that."

But I tried it anyhow because I seen he wanted me to. I went over to Lieutenant Bridges and said, "Why dont we just wait over until tomorrow? Maybe then . . ."

"No excuse, sir," he said. Then he turned and looked at me and said, "Look, who's the pilot around here? I am, aint I? You go on and take the train if you dont want to fly with me. Me, I fly, that's what I do. Off we go into the wild blue yonder. Put those cowlings on back there. Snap it up now. Snap. Snap. Snap."

So I seen there warnt any use in talking to him any longer, so I went over and tried to talk to Lieutenant Gar-

della but I dont think he even heered me. He was setting there blinking his eyes and I talked at him a while, only he didnt answer, and finally I reached down and waved my hand in front of his face, but he still just set there, staring ahead and blinking. So then I climbed up in the plane to try to talk to some of the others, only Lieutenant Kendall was already asleep; and I couldnt get Lieutenant Cover to pay no attention to me because he was already navigating just as hard as he could, writing and slinging maps around and peeping down tubes and things, and every time I said something to him, he told me to go away, he was busy.

So I finally give it up and went back outside to where Ben was setting under the tail and told him there didnt seem to be much way of stopping them, but that Lieutenant Bridges had said we could go back on the train ifn we wanted to. But Ben shook his head and said, "We just cant *do* that, Will!"

"How you mean we cant . . ."

"We cant," he said. "We're supposed to stay with the plane and you know that as good as I do. We cant just get off and take a train back every time something comes up. You know better than that, Will. You go ahead if you want to, but myself, I'll stick with the plane like I'm supposed to."

I never seen him so firm in my life—he didnt argue or get mad or nothing; he just said it and finally got up and walked away, still shaking his head, and wouldnt even discuss it with me no more.

So I didnt know what to do. I seen he didnt want to go but there warnt no way of talking him out of it. The mechanics was still trying to get the cowlings back on the engine, and Lieutenant Bridges strutted around and yelled out orders at them. I went over and set down on one of the

wheels of the plane and started rolling a cigarette, but then I thought about being too close to the engines to smoke, but then I got to thinking that it wouldnt be such a bad idea if they did blow up so I went ahead and lit it and puffed real hard and flipped ashes this way and that, but nothing ever come of it. They finally got the cowlings back on and Lieutenant Bridges was raring to go, prancing around and waving his arms and saying, "Snap it up. Snap. Snap. Snap," and things like that, and finally the mechanics moved the stand, and I heered one of them say, "We ought to report it to Operations," and the other answer, "He'll be gone before we have a chance. There aint a truck around."

Anyhow, what happened was, Lieutenant Bridges started going around the plane yelling, "All aboard!" and making noises like a train with his mouth, and then he thought of that old joke about, "Get aboard, and if you cant get aboard, get a plank!" and he yelled that one out a lot of times, and everybody that warnt in started getting in; and I decided I would ride up front again and watch them some more. It was real interesting to me up there, and I thought with them all drunk that way, it would be *especially* interesting, so I yelled to Ben just as he was climbing in that I was going to ride up front, and then I went to get the chocks out from under the wheel. But when I got back, Lieutenant Bridges had already slammed the door, and when I started to knocking on it, trying to get in, I heered one of the engines trying to start.

So for a minute there, I didnt know what to do. I beat some more and nobody opened up, and then one of the engines started backfiring like an old car trying to start up and took my cap off, so I decided to run around to the back and

try to get in there. But then that door was locked too and about that time, another one of the engines started with the wind blowing back so that I had to lean into it to keep from falling, so then I run around to the side of the blister to yell at Ben to come unlock the door for me. But about that time another one of the engines started sputtering and taking on, and then the plane give a lurch and jumped forward, and stopped, and then lurched again, and started taxiing off down the runway, so all I could do was just start running and take off after it.

Anyhow, I had to run that way for the longest sort of time, waving my arms and yelling for Ben, trying to get his attention. I was right down under him, but he just set there in front of the blister holding on with his face pale and his eyes big, and all these straps tied around him. And the only way I ever did get him to look around was by slinging a handful of pebbles against the side of it, yelling out, "Ben, open the door! Open the door!" and running along making motions with my hand to show him what I was talking about.

So then he started trying to get up, but that took him a pretty long time because of the way he had these straps fixed on him. He had little locks around and about, and straps coming down over his shoulder, the way he said jet pilots fixed theirselves in their cockpits, and I thought he never would get them all off. The plane kept on bobbing up and down, going down the runway with the engines backfiring, and I kept running along trying to keep up, and it looked like to me Ben had to undo fifteen straps before he could even move. And then I seen him lean over and start undoing some around his feet. But he finally made it, just as the

plane was stopping down at the end of the runway to rev up the engines, and I seen him get up; and in a second after that, the door opened.

Anyhow, what happened then, I started to climb in, but Ben held out his hand for me, so I took it and was just ready to pull myself up when the plane bobbed and the tail end went up in the air and I slipped back. So instead of me getting *in*, Ben come sailing *out*. He come flying over my head, his feet going this way and that, and I hit right on my back and Ben kept going. And I guess he must have hit right hard because he didnt even know what was going on for a while after that; he just set there shaking his head like he was trying to come to again.

And before I could do anything else, there was this big roar from the engines and it started to move. It went off bumping and twisting and bucking like a wild horse with the plane straining to get up off the runway like a big buzzard reaching out and feeling of the air with its wings. It got a few feet up and slammed back down so you could see the wheels squash down under the weight, and then all of a sudden it kind of hopped right up off the ground and went zooming along with its right wing going down until it nearly touched the runway. Then it wobbled back and forth until it was about a hundred feet high, and then it wiggled a few more times and straightened out and tried to climb, but then it just keeled over and up, so to speak. And when it hit the ground with the tail end flying off and burning, I was right glad we hadnt been in it after all. I mean something like that could *kill* you, probably, if you were in it. The front end didnt look so bad; it just went barreling on down the way without no tail until it hit this fence and stopped, but the back end had so much smoke and

fire around it, you couldnt even see it hardly. I mean it looked pretty dangerous that way, and I guess a lot of other folks thought so too because in a minute I heered sirens all over the place, wailing and screaming, and folks running across the runway and everything else.

So to tell you the truth, when I seen what happened to that back end, the way it was burning and everything, I really didnt care that me and Ben didnt make it. I didnt say nothing like that to Ben of course, but that's just the way I felt about it.

19

Anyhow, Ben was still kind of stunned a little bit, shaking his head and blinking his eyes, and I couldnt see no sense in going down to the plane with so many people around already, so what I done, I led him along until we got to the gate, and then I got us on this bus going into town. I figgered I would just head on down for the depot and get up on the train and head on back, but when we got to town, Ben was still kind of groggy from the fall and everything, so I took him up to a bench in the park and we set around there for a while, waiting for him to get cleared up.

But after he did get to feeling better, I kind of wished I had gone on to the depot in the first place, because then he started worrying pretty bad about everything. He started talking about how he bet Lieutenant Bridges and them was all killed and everything, and he got all down in the dumps about it no matter what I said. I told him it didnt look like to me they got hurt none, and he finally agreed it was possible they warnt, but he was still down a good bit, and had to worry about *something* it seemed like, so then he got started on what we was going to do and everything, and picked around that for a while; and then he hit on the idea that we didnt have no passes and here we were off the base, and that give him something to really tie into. He finally got right upset about it and said to me with his eyes right big, "Do you know what that makes us, Will? Off the base with no passes? That makes us Absent Without Leave, just as sure as anything. We're AWOL, Will! We're AWOL!"

So I seen it was better him having something to sink his teeth into that way, so I said, "Well, I guess that's a fact all right. I hadnt thought of it. It's true we aint got no passes."

"You doggone well right we dont!" Ben said. "We're just about the same as *deserters* when you come down to it. We were supposed to have stayed with the airplane!"

So I said I had never thought of it that way, and he said there warnt no other way to think of it. He said it was just as clear as anything, and then he got to talking about the Articles of War and things like that, and how nothing was no worse than running off and leaving your plane after it went down, and made a pretty big case out of it. He got to pacing up and down, saying this was probably the worst mess we had ever been in, and the least they would do was to send

us to prison, and how he wished we had stayed on the plane in the first place.

"Well, that was my fault, Ben," I said. "I was the one that made the mistake about that. I caused you to fall."

But Ben said, "That dont make any difference. Ignorance is no excuse, and we left the plane and it's a disgrace any way you look at it." And he stayed pretty firm about it too.

And after that, he got right hard on us, and was so dead-set on the idea that we was AWOL, he couldnt think of anything else. He stopped and set down and shook his head all miserable and said, "Here we are alive and they are all probably dead and . . . Oh, my, Will, we got to *do* something! And there cant be any slip-ups on it neither because we've done enough wrong as it is. We've got to do something quick!"

So I said why didnt we take the train on back then, but he had got up and was pacing again by that time, looking all worried and everything. He done that a while and finally got to nodding his head a little bit, and then he come over and set back down on the bench and said, "Look, Will, I've thought of a way, but I dont know whether we can use it or not. We've got to have some kind of organization from now on—that's been the trouble all along—so what we have to do now is use the plan of whoever is in *charge*. Now I've got a plan, but I dont know whether we can use it or not because . . ."

"Why, sho we can use it, Ben. *You* be in charge and we can use your plan and everything will work out fine, I bet. I aint got a plan nohow—all I was going to do was get on the train and go back."

But Ben said, "My goodness, Will, you cant just do things

169

like that. You cant just *put* somebody in charge that way. You're supposed to decide by date of rank. What's your date of rank now? That's how we decide."

"My what?"

"Your date of rank. We have to decide which one ranks the other before we know who will be in charge, and whose plan to use. That's the only way to work things right, Will."

So he had me there and I didnt know how to answer. So finally I just said, "Now, Ben, how are we ever going to figger anything like that? How is either one of us going to rank the other when we're both *recruits*. Why dont we just go ahead and use your plan and . . ."

But Ben said, "That's why I want to know your date of *rank*, Will. What day was you sworn in?"

"Why, the same day you was, Ben. You remember that. We . . ."

"But what time?" Ben said. "What *time* was you sworn in?"

"Well, I dont remember exactly what *time* it was, Ben. Look, let's just use your plan and you be in charge because I aint got one nohow. I was just . . ."

But Ben said, "Nosir. You'll have to get up a plan if you rank me because then you'll be in charge. Think. Try to remember."

So I thought back on it and finally it come to me. I remembered I was one of the first ones sworn in that day, and I was just about to say so when I caught myself and said, "Dont you remember what time you got sworn in?"

"Three-thirty-five that afternoon," Ben said.

"Well, I guess you are it," I said, "because I was one of the last ones that afternoon, I guess it was close to five o'clock."

So that done it all right. Ben decided he was in charge and

we could use his plan, and it turned out to be a mighty good plan too. You could tell he had give it a lot of thought and everything. He said the only thing for us to do would be to turn ourselves in, because that way, they wouldnt court-martial us so bad. But if we let them catch us, they would think we were trying to escape. "So the best way to manage it," he said, "is to sneak back out to the field as soon as it gets dark and climb over the fence and turn ourselves in down at Operations. We never should have left in the first place."

"Well, that was my fault," I said. "I was the one that got us on the bus and all."

"Rightfully, it aint," Ben said. "If I'm in charge, I have to take full responsibility for everything you do."

Anyhow, it was a right good plan once you thought on it a while. Myself, I couldnt see why we couldnt just walk up to the gate and say, "Here we is," but Ben had worked that out too. He said if we done that, they would know we had been off the base and could get us for being AWOL because we didnt have no passes. But if we climbed over the fence and sneaked in, they wouldnt even know we had been off the base. "As far as they would know," he said, "we might have just been wandering around the base all the time, out by the plane or somewheres. They wouldnt have no way of knowing we had been off the base at all; then they couldnt get us for being AWOL, at *least*. And I think that would be fair because we didnt really *mean* to go AWOL—not that that's much of an excuse, though. Anyhow, dont that make sense to you, Will?"

And once I thought on it some more, I guess it did all right. The way he had figgered it and wiggled it around, it seemed about the *only* thing to do, so it really was a good

plan once you understood it. So I said I was all for it and told him how glad I was that he was in charge because I never would have thought up nothing like that, and he got to feeling some better about things. He said, "Well, I guess we had better get at it then. We cant just sit around here in the park all day talking about it. If we're going to hide out until dark, we had better get started with it."

And he couldnt have picked no better time to get started with it because just about time he said it, I looked up and seen these two AP's headed right for us. I punched Ben right quick and started to tell him that it looked like we was going to be caught even before we got started, but then he started making all these motions for me to shut up, which I done right quick, and then he started doing some more quick planning. He held his lips real tight so they wouldnt move and said to me without looking, "Just act casual, Will. Dont say nothing or do nothing until I give the word, and act real casual."

And then he kind of leaned back on the bench like he was real lazy and everything, and begun acting real casual and all. And he really done a job on it too. The AP's was headed right for us when I heered this noise and looked around and seen that Ben was *humming* to himself, and humming real *loud* too. I started to shush him, but then I seen he was acting casual, so I just tried to do like he done, only I never was able to come nowheres close to the way Ben was doing. He had leaned back and flung one arm over the side of the bench and propped his foot up on the side of it, and then he took to stretching and yawning and things like that until I thought he was going to fall off the bench. And then he said to me, real loud so the AP's could hear, half-yawning when he said it, "Well, I guess we had better

head on for town, *Thompson,*" and then he got up and stretched some more. So I got up and done the same, and then we headed on down the walk to the left of the AP's, not right *at* them or *away* from them, but just a little to the *left* of them, and both of us just kind of strolled along, like we was just sauntering, so to speak. Ben whispered to me, "Just dont look at them now. Just keep on with me," and then he yawned some more and a lot of other things like that. I guess it was about the best job of acting casual I ever seen in my life, and I think the AP's must have thought so too because both of them stopped after a bit, and watched us all the rest of the way out of the park.

Anyhow, we got out all right that way and headed toward town, sticking to the back streets, and I took on a good bit about the way Ben had done. I said, "You really put it over on them fine, Ben. You really done a job that time," and stuff like that, but Ben said, "Yeah, but the day aint over yet, you remember. We've got a long ways to go yet."

So we went on down the street and kind of dodged in buildings every once in a while and come out on the other side, and things like that. We would be walking along and Ben would say, "Cross here," and we'd cross real quick and get to the other side, and then head back in the direction we was coming from. We done a lot of things like that, in and out of stores and crossing streets and changing directions, and went on that way until I was getting right wore out from it, and Ben was too. So then Ben got the idea of hiding out somewhere and resting a bit, which sounded right good to me until he started explaining how it would be best to go out somewhere and find a house and crawl up under it for the rest of the day, and I really warnt too much for that because it seemed too hot for something like that

the rest of the day. I said, "Why dont we just go to a restaurant or a drugstore or something like that, where they got fans?"

But Ben said, "You cant hide in a place like that."

"Well, I dont think it would be taking *too* much of a chance, Ben. We aint even *seen* an AP for the past two hours now, and it seems like to me . . ."

"This way," Ben said, starting off, "I'll be thinking about it as we move along. You dont want to just stand here and talk about it."

So we went on up another street and crossed back and then started down an alley where there was a lot of these big tin garbage cans setting around, and the first thing I knowed, Ben was eyeing them right hard. And that kind of bothered me because I didnt care a thing about spending the afternoon in one of them cans as hot as it was, so I got to saying right quick that it was about the hottest day I ever seen, and all like that, but he kept on eyeing them; and I guess before it was over, that's where we would have hid out all right if we hadnt of come out of that alley just where we did. But then he looked up and pointed across the street and said all of a sudden, "That's it, Will. A picture show. It'll be dark and cool in there and we can move from seat to seat, and nobody would ever think to pick us up there. I dont know why I didnt think of that before."

"Me neither," I said. "And that's what I call real hiding out. A picture show . . ."

So we went in and had a right nice time there. It was cool and they had candy and popcorn in the lobby and a machine where you could get drinks and things, and the seats was comfortable enough to nod in, and besides that, they had this dogged good movie on about the Air Force and things. It

was about these folks that was all out to conquer the air and it showed them zooming off in these planes every few minutes, talking over the interphones and sweating and calling out to each other about fuel valves and cowl flaps and a lot of stuff like that. And there was this woman in it who was in the tower talking to the pilot over the radio and she kept yelling about cowl flaps and things like that too, but then he went into this steep dive *anyhow* while everybody stood around talking about the landing gear and fuel valves and things, but he pulled out of it all right and zoomed around some more, and then he landed and walked kind of slow up toward the tower, and this woman, she done a good job of not crying no more, and then he reached up and took this cigarette out of his mouth and flipped it away and give a little salute with his hand, and this woman kept holding her lips tight together and all like that while they kept walking right head on at each other; and after that they had this comedy about Popeye and it was mighty good too.

So we hid out there for the rest of the afternoon, changing seats every once in a while, so as not to stay in any one place too long, and every once in a while we went out to the lobby to get something to eat, and it was one of the best hideout places I ever seen.

20

We stayed there until about eight o'clock when Ben decided that it was time to go. "It'll be about time they're changing guards," he said. "And who'll ever think about somebody slipping in at eight o'clock at night? We'll get them by surprise."

So then we headed back for the field. Ben didnt want to take a bus or a taxi or nothing because we had to slip in, so we had to walk it. Only Ben didnt want to go down the sidewalk, so we went up and down alleys and through back yards and across lawns until we finally made it to the outside of town. But then we didnt know where we was and couldnt get ourselves located, and finally had to go ask somebody; we found out then that we was on the wrong side of town, so we caught a taxi and went back to the middle and started all over again.

By that time, it was about ten o'clock, but Ben still wanted to go back through the alleys again, so we done that, only this time we kept the main road in sight so that we wouldnt get lost any more. We got to the end of town and then headed out across some fields toward the beacon light that swung around and made flashes in the sky. We stayed away from the highway so that it made it right hard going as the fields was covered with bushes and this high wire grass that come up to about my waist. But we creeped along that way

real easy, trying to be quiet and all; but that was right hard to do in that grass as there was holes in the ground that we stumbled in every once in a while so that sometimes Ben's head would go right out of sight when he went down in one; and the grass was right thick so you had to fight your way through it some of the time. We went along about a mile like that, though, with Ben whispering, "Easy now. Easy and quiet," and thrashing around in the grass trying to get through tangles of it, making so much noise most of the time that I couldnt even hear him whispering to me.

Anyhow, we was still about two miles from the field so all you could see of it was the beacon light and the barracks lights and things, but he still wanted it quiet, and we thrashed along like that for a while longer until we got close enough for the beacon light to flash on us as it went by. It would come swinging around at us, getting brighter and brighter, and then Ben would hiss at me, "Watch it!" and we'd stoop down in the grass and let it swing by us, going for another round again. And after that, we'd stoop down each time it come around, then get up and make some headway, then stoop back down again; and we bobbed up and down like that for about another mile, I guess, until I was getting right wore out with it and Ben was too.

And by that time, Ben decided that we was so close now that we had better stay stooped over all the rest of the way and just crawl along. So we done that for a while, but that was a little too wearing on both of us, so Ben decided that we could bob up and down some more, and try to make time whenever the beacon passed over our heads. It would come by and go over us and then we'd start thrashing along again, and then have to fall flat when it come back. But we kept that up until we made this one dash for it that took

us within about fifty yards of the fence, and Ben dived and hit in the grass next to me and was so wore out he couldnt get up for the next dash at all. He set there panting and puffing in the grass, and I done the same, letting the beacon go around a few times without even moving. Along the highway on the side, you could see the cars going along the road with their headlights stuck out, and over the fence you could see the barracks lighted up; but where we was, it was dark and quiet, and I was kind of enjoying resting there a little bit.

And Ben was too; he kept puffing and panting and taking on, and said, "Dogged if I aint about done for. I dont know whether I can make it over that fence, or not."

"Well, maybe you wont have to climb over it," I said. "If I can just pull up the wire on the bottom, you can just crawl under."

But Ben said, "No, we'll have to go one at a time. It'll be safer that way. First, though, one of us ought to sneak along the edge of the fence and see where they got the guards posted."

"I'll do that," I said. "You just rest."

So I got up and started down there, but then I heered Ben hissing at me again and went back; and he said I couldnt just go walking up to the fence that way, that I had to crawl to keep from being seen. So I told him I just forgot, and then I got down and started crawling through the grass again. I crawled about a hundred yards down on one side, right close up to the fence, and didnt see a soul nowhere, and then I crawled back to Ben and told him there warnt nobody around even within shouting distance. But he said, "Yeah, but how about on the other side?" so then I crawled back down that way a bit and still didnt see a guard no-

where, and by that time my knees was about wore out, so I finally just got up and walked back toward where Ben was, but I seen him waving at me so frantic that I finally got back down and crawled some more. But when I got back, I told him there warnt nobody around and started to roll myself a cigarette, but he said, "Hey, dont do that. You strike a match out here and we're done for. It might mess everything up. We got to be careful."

So I opened the pouch up and put the tobacco back, and we set there a while longer until Ben said, "I guess we can make a run for it now. We'll have to time that light just right and then skeedaddle, and I dont mean maybe." He was squatted down, peering over the top of the grass this way and that. "I'll go first," he said. "If I make it, you follow me, and if I dont make it, you take off and go around the other side of the field and try it there. Dont bother with me if I get caught. You just take off on your own."

"Why, Ben, I wouldnt do that. I . . . ."

"That's the way it is," Ben said. "If they get me, I'll cause enough trouble so they wont notice you, and you might be able to make it all right. You understand that now? You just take off and forget about me."

"Now, Ben, I aint going to do nothing like that! I dont . . ."

But Ben snapped out at me, "That's enough. Those are my *orders.*"

So I seen then that he was having a right big time of it, so I begun to join in a little bit. I got down and peered this way and that like he was doing, and I done a lot of whispering, and all that kind of stuff. And then I made out all sorts of things—I made out I could hear the guards talking right close up, and Ben listened and thought he heered them

too. He said, "Duck!" and fell down flat, and I did too; then he come raising up real slow listening again; and then I made out I heered them *behind* us, and Ben listened hard and whispered, "Take it easy now," and stuff like that; and then I made out I heered hound dogs barking and people yelling and guns shooting and a lot of things like that, but he didnt like that too much; he said, "Will, what's the matter with you? You dont hear all that stuff and you know it!"

So I said I must have been mistaken, and after a little bit, Ben got up ready to make his run for it. I said, "Ben, you sho you dont want me to come along and pull up the wire and just let you climb under?" but he shushed me again. He squatted and peered around, ducking his head when the light come over, and then he started running for it. I set there in the grass watching him; I seen him go thrashing through the grass and get to the fence and give a lunge at it and go scampering up it like a cat going up a tree. Then the light went around and I couldnt see him no more, and then the light come back and I seen him up near the top of the fence with one foot caught in the wire, snatching at it trying to get it loose. Then the light went around again and I couldnt see him for a while, only hear him pulling and snatching, and when it come by the next time, he was right on the top of the fence and had somehow managed to get *both* feet hung in the wire. So I heered all kinds of racket as he snatched this way and that, and then I seen him outlined against the sky just about the time he lost his balance —both hands flew straight up over his head and one foot come loose and went slinging out in the air like he was kicking at something; then the light was gone and I couldnt see

him no more. But I could *hear* him right clear when he fell because when he hit it sounded something like a big tree coming down out in the woods somewhere.

Anyhow, he was out like a light when I got to him; he had fell right on the back of his neck and warnt stirring at all. He was still breathing all right, though, and I couldnt find nothing broke nowhere; he was just out for a while and that was all.

So I figgered with him out that way, that put me in charge and I had to use my plan, only I didnt have much of one, and the only thing I could think of was to pick him up and start toward the highway. I flagged down a taxi going along and told him Ben was drunk and to take us to the train station; and when we got there, I took Ben in the rest room and went through his pockets, getting all our money together, which come to only eleven dollars and fifty-five cents. And then I went up to the window to get the tickets back, only I didnt have anywhere near enough money, so finally I just told the fellow to give me two tickets in that direction, so we could at least get started anyhow. Then I went back and splashed some water on Ben's face to wake him up, and told him what I had done, but he didnt have much to say about it. He had been knocked out *twice* that day, though, so I guess he warnt much up to thinking about it by then.

So finally I helped him out to one of the benches in the waiting room and he set there rubbing at his neck, still not feeling too good. We had only thirty cents left after the tickets, but I finally decided it was best I go ahead and spend some on some coffee for him so he could get his head cleared back up again. So I brought it back to him and he set there

sipping it; and I waited for his head to clear back up again so he could do some more thinking, and be back in charge again.

21

But Ben was still right dazed for a while after we got on the train, and he was right miserable too about everything, I think. I got him a seat next to the window and he set there rubbing his neck and not saying anything because he was right down on things by then—he wanted things done right and he didnt like them done no other way, and there warnt no in-between for him. Either it was done correct for Ben or it warnt done correct, there warnt no four or five ways about it. But he was too wore out with everything by then to even get upset over it; he tried some but finally he just laid his head over against the window, and the next thing I knowed, he was dead asleep again, his mouth open, snoring, his head drooped down on his chest.

So I figgered I would go ahead and try to work things out before he woke up so he wouldnt have that to worry with and I got up and went down to the wash room where I had seen some folks going in, thinking maybe I could find the

conductor and see if there warnt some way me and Ben could work on the train or something in return for some tickets the rest of the way to Martinville. Anyhow the conductor warnt down there but there was a fellow with a guitar sitting over in the corner strumming at it, so I sat down and listened to him for a bit and kind of got to enjoying it. He was pretty good on it, I thought. There was a blind man with a beard sitting in there too and then a fellow come in with a juice harp, and we had a right good time of it. They got to going together on a few songs and the blind man started patting his foot up and down and got right excited about it, letting the tobacco drip down over his beard while he tried to hum along with the music, making noises down in his throat; and then me and him got together on a couple of them. We done "Honky-Tonking" with the blind fellow singing most of it and me just coming in a little bit on the chorus, and then we made a duet out of it. They'd play the first part and he'd yell out, "If you got the money, honey," and I'd come in on: "I've got the ti-hi-hime!" and then we'd both sing the last part together: "We'll go honky-tonking and have a great big time!" and then we'd go back and do the other part all together, so we had a nice time on that one until we done it two or three more times and kind of wore it out. But then we done that one that goes: "That little ole chile of Galilee!" and he'd sing that part and I'd come in on the "Dee, dee, di, dee!" and he'd holler out, "Yessir, that little ole chile of Galilee!" and I'd hit the other part, and we had a right big time on that one until we switched around and I done the part about the little ole chile of Galilee, and he kind of got too excited on the other part and throwed back his head and went, *"Dee, dee, di, dee!"* and mighty near swallowed his plug of tobacco he

had in his mouth and kept choking for the longest sort of time before we found out he warnt still singing and hit him on the back a few times to keep him from strangling to death.

We got him some water and he got all right again, and then I borrowed a mouth organ off the boy that had the juice harp and done the Fox Hunt for them and put in the baying of the hounds and the hunters and the horses and all like that; and by that time the old man had rested up some and said had we ever heered anybody go like a train with their feet. Well, I had, and I guess the others had too, but we all said No, and he got up and got to shuffling his feet around, back and forth, getting faster and faster with it until he really was doing it pretty good, except that I have heered it done better, but not no better by a blind man, I dont think. Anyhow, he was getting into it pretty good making the whistles and the sounds and all like that with his mouth when the conductor stuck his head in and told him he was waking everybody up, and that made him kind of mad and he cussed the conductor and the conductor cussed him back, and then he drawed back and spit a whole mouthful of tobacco all the way across the room but missed the conductor and hit the boy with the juice harp on the side of the face instead, which made the boy kind of mad so that he got riled up and said he'd seen folks do that train thing a lot better than the blind man had done it; anyhow they got to arguing some about it so me and the fellow with the guitar got to going on "Just a Little Walk with Jesus," which kind of settled them down again, so then I got up and excused myself and went back to look for the conductor like I had started off to do in the first place.

Anyhow, I went back and found the conductor in another

car so I went up and told him how it was that me and Ben had to go all the way to Martinville and didnt have money enough to make it and what did he think was the best thing for us to do about it, and all like that, and talked to him a good while about it. And he was mighty nice about it too. He said, "Well, you know, that certainly is a coincidence because I remember one time when I was in the 342nd Infantry and me and some boys went into Paris on leave, and we was coming back, only we didnt have enough money for tickets all the way neither, and . . . why dont you set down here, young fellow? I dont get to talk to many service men nowadays nohow . . ." So we shook hands and I set down across from him and we had a nice long chat about when he was in Paris which was a right long story that lasted for nearly an hour, I guess. And it was right interesting too, only the fellow kind of leaned over talking to you and got his face up about a foot from yourn and got his head to bobbing around so that after a while you couldnt see nothing but just the outline of him, and hear his voice way off somewheres. But he kept on, saying, "Yessir, I like to help out a service man when I have a chance because I remember one time when I was in London, and I always had guard duty there, it seemed like, and we used to have this dog we kept around the post and took him on guard duty with us, and this dog had a head that was too big for his body, and I believe that it was the biggest head I ever seen on a dog in my life because when he was standing still, the head would start going down and the tail would start coming up and the first thing you knowed, its head would be resting on the ground and the tail would be about a foot up in the air with his legs just dangling there, and one night when I was on guard duty, I had this here dog out there with me and . . ." and he

went on like that for about another hour until I got so dizzy I almost couldnt think and couldnt keep up with the rest of it at all. And then I got to feeling like I couldnt move somehow, but after a while he reached out and slapped me on the shoulder, which kind of brought me to again.

Anyhow, he said it was mighty nice being able to talk with a service man again, and all like that, and was real polite about it, and then he wanted me to go along with him while he made his round on the train. So I went along, and he told me about this and that, and about a lot of other things he done in the service, and after we got through making the rounds, he took me back to another one of the train men and said, "Charlie, I want you to meet a service man." So me and Charlie shook hands for a while and talked a bit too; he said he had a cousin in the army by the name of Dan Baker and did I know him? and I said I didnt, and he said that Dan was in the Third Army Division, and I said I still didnt believe I knowed him, and he told me what all Dan looked like and said he knowed good and well that Dan was in, but I still didnt know him, so he finally got kind of mean about it and said he doubted if Dan would know me either.

So anyhow we talked with Charlie for a while, and then the conductor took me back to another fellow and pointed to me and said I was a service man, and this other fellow was a little mean-looking, narrow-faced man, and he said he knowed it and went on off; so then me and the conductor went off to talk some more, only I couldnt set at it long this time because something kept happening to my eyes so I couldnt see too good with his head bobbing up and down in front of you that way, so finally I asked him if he wouldnt like to meet Ben because Ben's daddy was a soldier too, and he said, "Oh, an old military family, eh?" and we

186

went back and woke Ben up and the conductor set down, and I got a little bit of rest for a while.

And I guess I must have dozed off because when I woke up it was already daylight; there was red in the east where the sun was coming up and the man was still talking even though he was right hoarse by this time, but he was still going at it with his face poked right up in Ben's, and when I got a look at Ben, I felt kind of bad about going off to sleep like that because he looked about as bad as I ever seen him. His eyes was kind of glazed something like a fish's eyes, and his neck was twisted sideways and his mouth was hanging open, and for a minute there, I didnt think I was going to be able to get him out of it because he kept setting and staring that way even after the man stopped talking at him. But I reached over and shook him and finally his eyes come back to focus, and then I got started on how we had to figger out something to do. I said, "Look, it's nearly day already and it's about time for us to get off. And we got to figger out some way to make out the rest of the way. We been riding this train nearly five hours now and . . ."

"Five hours," the conductor said. "Well, as for myself I been riding this train thirty-two years now and I guess in thirty-two years ifn you stop and figger it out, well that come to quite a few hours altogether . . ."

So then he started figgering out how many trips he had made in thirty-two years and how many hours that would be; he got out his pencil and paper and started working on it, explaining just how he was figgering it, and I seen then that he was going to get started again, so I figgered I would go back to the rest room a minute and come back and try to get him onto something else so I could find out something, only he got up and followed me when I left with his pencil and

187

paper wanting to know how old I was. And when I told him he started figgering to see if he had spent more time on the train than I had been alive, and then he started figgering how much he made per hour and then how much he would have made if he had of made ten cents more per hour, and how much all that come to; he followed me along down to the rest room and I listened as much as I could because it looked to me after he got through with that one he would have to slow down a while because he was so hoarse by then, you could barely make out what he said; and I think it would have worked that way too, only when we come into the room, he was still talking and woke up the blind man who was setting in the corner so that he took another long shot at him and hit right on the paper the man was figgering on. It was about as good spitting as I ever seen a blind man do in my life, but it made the conductor kind of mad and he got to fussing around about it, and when I asked him, "What do you think we ought to do about getting on to Martinville?" he turned around and looked at me and said, "How do *I* know what you ought to do? Why dont you git off the train and git a job and make some money or something?" and turned around and stomped on out of the place and wouldnt even talk about it no more.

And so that's what we done, once the train stopped. We got off and I found a job that day pushing a wheelbarrow and Ben kept count of the number I had to push; and it took us six whole days before we ever got up money enough to buy another ticket.

22

Anyhow, when we got back there that next Saturday, there warnt nobody around. It was as empty as I ever seen it in my life. We caught the bus out to the field from town, me and Ben the only ones on it, and when we got off we didnt see nobody, and I think Ben kind of halfway got it in his head that they was probably all out hunting for us. After the bus left, he stood around looking up and down the streets, not seeing nobody, and his face got right pale. The only thing we even seen alive was this old dog laying on the steps in front of the post office. Ben kept looking around saying, "I wonder where everybody is. They couldnt have all gone on passes at the same time, it dont seem like," and he kind of whispered it when he said it, because it *was* a funny kind of feeling coming back to a place where there was usually lots of folks around and not see a soul. It made everything kind of lonesome and quiet and peculiar feeling.

Anyhow, we stood around like that for a while, and then decided to head on down to the Orderly Room, and we went on down street after street, not seeing a soul. I mean there warnt nobody around the PX or the drill field or nowhere, and the only sound you could hear was the footsteps you were taking; and you couldnt hear much of that neither because before we had gone a couple of blocks, we was both kind of tiptoeing along.

Anyhow, we were kind of creeping along that way down next to the hangars when we heered this bellow that would mighty near knock your ears out. It blared out, *"Ten-shun!"* so loud that it seemed to be just hanging in the air, and Ben froze right where he was standing. He give a gasp and come to attention and I done the same, and we both just *stood* there for a second. I mean there warnt a soul around nowhere and when we heered that bellow, it was pretty much of a shock all right. Ben stood there stiff at attention with his eyes about double their usual size, and I done the same.

But then all of a sudden, the noise started blaring again, saying this time: *"Attention to orderrrrrs!* Thirty-Eighty-oh-Ninth Training Wing, by Orders of the Commanding Officer!" and some more stuff like that with the words just echoing out in the air; and about that time Ben said to me, "It's on the other side of the hangars. It's . . ." and stopped and listened again. "It's a parade, by gosh! That was just the loud-speaker, that's all. Come on, Will, inside the hangar—we can see it from there!"

So we took off and run inside the hangar and climbed up on some boxes to look out, and there was the whole field out there on the ramp in formation. I never seen so many of them in my life, and they was mighty good to see too.

"My Gosh," Ben said, "that really is a parade, aint it?"

Then about that time the band struck up with the drums going and everything and this fellow that had been bellowing over the loud-speaker turned and started walking real fast with his chest poked out past the window and on down toward the reviewing stand where we couldnt see him no more. Ben kept looking this way and that, saying, "I never seen such a crowd of people! Come on, let's go over to the other window so we can see the reviewing stand!"

So we scrambled down off of those boxes and went over to the other window and scrambled up some more, and from there we was looking right down on the platform. "Look, Will," Ben said. "There's the Commanding Officer and there's another Colonel, and looker there, Will: There's a General! And who is that other one, I wonder . . ."

"I never seen him before."

"It's the *Mayor*," Ben said, all excited about it. "Sho it is. I've seen his pictures in the paper and look . . . *look* . . ." and then he stopped all of a sudden. He looked at me with his mouth falling open, and then he looked back out again trying to point but just getting his hand about halfway up and just letting it dangle there, and then I seen what he was talking about. Because there they all were, standing there in a row so bandaged up you couldnt tell who they were at first—all four of them. There was Lieutenant Bridges with his head all bandaged up, and Lieutenant Gardella on a crutch, and Lieutenant Cover and Lieutenant Kendall, all of them wrapped up in so much gauze you wouldnt hardly know them. They was lined up there on the reviewing stand next to the General and the Mayor and the Commanding Officer. It was such a surprise to Ben that he just looked and looked and couldnt say a word for a minute. Then he turned to me with this big grin on his face, and then he looked back out again and the grin started coming off. Then it come back again, then went off again, so for a while there you couldnt make out *what* he thought. He seemed mighty glad *they* was alive, but not so glad that *he* was. He started to say something, but about that time the band struck up and then there was some more talking over the loud-speaker, and we seen Lieutenant Bridges and Lieutenant Gardella and them

filing down off the stand and walking in front of it. And then the General stepped down there with them holding a piece of paper in his hand; then some other people followed and there was a lot of picture-taking and so on while Lieutenant Bridges and them tried to stand at attention with all them bandages and crutches and things. And then the General stepped up to the loud-speaker and started talking, and I mean it was something to listen to. Ben looked at me with his face kind of funny, and said, "They are going to decorate them, Will! Listen to that! Listen. . . ."

And it was worth listening to, too. The General got to reading off this paper some of the most powerful sounding words I ever heered, all about how the Air Force was mighty proud to have such men as they was, and how it was because of such men that we had the greatest Air Force in the world, and all such things as that. He took on about it until there just seemed there warnt nothing else he could say about them; so then he started back and went through it again, and then after he wore that out, he got started on them one at a time. He called out Lieutenant Bridges' name and said how it was that Lieutenant Bridges had landed the plane and had helped to pull the co-pilot out of the burning wreckage of the airplane, and how this reflected glory on himself and on the Air Force too, and so on like that. It was really something to hear too. It made you proud just thinking that you *knowed* such a man by the time he got through with him. I turned to Ben to say so, but his face was all wrinkled up again, and then I heered him mumbling, "That's right too, because he done it too, and he deserves it. Because he stayed there and we run off like cowards and . . ."

"Ben, that aint so! You aint no coward and besides I was the one that got us on that bus and . . ."

"Listen," Ben said, looking out the window again. "He's going to get started again."

So I looked back out just as the General was beginning to take on over Lieutenant Gardella, and this time he kept at it a good while too. He said a lot of good things about him and went on to tell how it was that he had gone back in the plane and pulled Lieutenant Cover out of the burning wreckage after Lieutenant Bridges had pulled *him* out, and how this was beyond the call of duty and how it reflected glory and all: and then he got to going on Lieutenant Cover and the way he navigated and how he pulled Lieutenant Kendall out of the burning wreckage, which was beyond the call of duty too: and then he started in on Lieutenant Kendall who didnt pull nobody out of the burning wreckage but who at least went back in the plane *to* pull somebody out, only there warnt nobody else to pull out, which warnt his fault, so he had done things beyond the call of duty too and had reflected some glory; and then he went on for a while longer that way saying things that you never would have thought could happen with them in the airplane. It made you right proud just to be amongst them when you stopped to think of them running in and out of that plane, pulling each other out, and I really would have been enjoying it ifn it hadnt of been for Ben, so miserable the way he was.

But he was hating himself a good bit, and when the General said, "In view of the boldness and daring of the above named officers who have reflected honor on themselves and on the Air Force, each of these officers is being awarded the Air Medal," I thought it was going to be too much for him.

The band struck up, and the General began stepping up to each one of them to pin the medal on, and I could hear Ben give a sigh each time he done it.

"An Air Medal!" Ben said. "Just like that! And we . . . we . . ."

"Yeah, Ben," I said, "but if we had of stayed in that plane, we would be dead and . . ."

But then Ben said, "Hush, listen . . ." because the General was stepping back up to the loud-speaker again. He tapped on it a couple of times with his finger and then he stood there a minute clearing his throat while some of the newspapermen took pictures of him, and then he pulled out this other piece of paper and got himself a deep breath, and got started up again. He went off slow at first, saying how he had some other medals to award and how he was proud to do it and all like that, just getting kind of warmed up; and the first thing I knowed he was talking about *us*. I looked at Ben and said, "Listen, Ben, he's . . ." but Ben already was; he waved his hand at me, and I turned back to listen, and by this time the General was going pretty strong too, taking on over me and Ben. And he really done a job of it too. It was a lot better than any of the rest of them—he said as how we had give our lives for our country which was about as far beyond the call of duty as you could *get,* and how we reflected glory on ourselves and on the Air Force, and practically everywhere else, and then that for Will Stockdale Deceased and Ben Whitledge Deceased, he didnt have just *one* medal, but *two,* the Air Medal and Purple Heart both!

And when I heered that I reached over and slapped Ben on the back and said, "Listen to that, will you? We got two

194

medals, Ben. We got two medals, and we aint even dead!"

But Ben begun shaking his head from side to side, saying, "No, we aint. Not really we aint. When they find out we aint dead . . ."

"When they find out, they'll probably give us one for pulling each *other* out, Ben. Why, doggit, you *know* they will!"

But he shook his head again and started climbing down off the box, saying, "There aint no use talking about it. We might as well go on back and get it over with."

So we climbed down and headed on back toward the Orderly Room with Ben looking so droopy, it's a wonder he could even make it. He just plodded along with his head hanging down, and when they started on another lively march with the drums going and everything, he didnt even try to keep in step with it.

23

I tried to perk Ben up by walking in step and strutting to the music and marching backward and all like that, but he wouldnt even look at me. So finally I cut that out and got to talking about how everybody was going to be surprised to see us, and how glad they was going to be to find out we was still alive, and all like that, thinking it might perk him up a

bit. I said, "Just wait until Sergeant King sees us. Wont that be something, though?" and I took on about it a good bit that way.

And it did come off pretty good there at first too. Sergeant King was so surprised when we came in through the door, he didnt even believe it for a few minutes. He was setting there reading a magazine with his feet propped up on the desk; and when we stepped in and I said, "Well, I bet you never expected to see us no more, but *here we air!*" he was so surprised, he wouldnt even look at us for a minute, and just kept setting that way for the longest sort of time before he finally come around to peeping over the top of his magazine at us. And then he let the magazine fall right out of his hands and leaned forward staring kind of popeyed at us, muttering under his breath, "Oh, my God! Oh, my God!"

So I said, "Didnt I tell you he would be surprised, Ben?" and Ben stepped up and said, "Will Stockdale and Ben Whitledge reporting for duty after a unforeseen delay," and said it real snappy, looking like he felt a lot better already.

But Sergeant King set there not answering or saying nothing for a while, just staring from one to the other with his feet still up on the desk and leaning forward so that he was bent about double, which was a right uncomfortable way of setting; but he stayed like that not saying nothing for the longest sort of time, and when he finally did come around to opening his mouth, he said in a real low, hoarse voice, *"Why aint yall dead?"* which really warnt much to say at all.

But I said, "We got on the train and come back. We was a little late because we ran out of money but we made it all right. We . . ."

"You aint dead," he said. "You aint dead . . ."

"I just told you," I said. "We . . ."

But he kept on staring that way, and said, "You aint dead and I'm the one that went down there and identified your remains and . . ."

"Well, that was just a mistake," I said. "Because we aint dead, no matter what you say, and . . ."

"Your dog tags was there," Sergeant King said. "I seen them and I seen some of your clothes and the whole tail end of that airplane was burned and I was the one that had to make the report and I thought . . ."

"Sho," I said. "I know what you thought because we was just down by the parade and . . ."

And then all of a sudden he hopped up and both feet hit the floor and he yelled out like he was about half-crazy, "The parade! The parade!"

"Now, look," I said. "That aint no way to act, is it? Here me and Ben is alive and you . . ."

But then he started looking this way and that like he didnt have good sense, and all of a sudden he started bounding across the room, and then stopped and come back, and then his eyes lighted up again, and he went bounding back across the room again heading for the door and calling out, "Lieutenant! Lieutenant!" and slamming the door right in our faces.

So I said to Ben, "Well, I wouldnt pay no attention to him. He's always acted kind of peculiar like that," because you could tell Ben was already getting worried. But then there was a lot of commotion and talking in the other room, and then all of a sudden the door flung open and the Lieutenant stood staring at us a second, and then he yelled out, "Dont move! Dont move!" and slammed the door again, which

197

made Ben jump. And then he opened it up again and yelled out, "If you move, I'll have you shot!" which mighty near scared him to death, it looked like.

I said, "Well, hit's just that they are kind of surprised right now. Later on, they'll be more glad to see us."

"There aint no telling what they'll do with us," Ben said. "If we'd have gotten in the infantry like I've wanted to all my life we'd never been in this mess. Now, like I say, there aint no telling *what* they'll do with us."

"Well, I wouldnt feel that way," I said. "It's just that they are kind of upset right now and later on after they get accustomed to it, I'll mention it to them about them medals and . . ."

But then the door flung open again and Sergeant King and the Lieutenant come out again, and this time they was talking awful rough, it seemed like. The Lieutenant lit into us again, wanting to know what we was doing alive, and I told him about it, and he raved around a few minutes, not making good sense, and then he started in on Sergeant King again, wanting to know all about it, and got right ornery about it before it was over. Sergeant King explained to him how he found the dog tags and some of our clothes and all like that, and told him how the back end of the plane was burned, and told him how he figgered we was dead, and all like that, but then the Lieutenant busted in on him, and said, "Sergeant King, you can say nearly anything you want to me, but if you explain to me one more time how you knew they were dead, that's going to be the end of you! Now you get to the General in a hurry and dont fool around about it —tell him to leave their names off the list. Tell him just not to mention them because they've got the newspapers down there and everybody else, including the Mayor—it's the only thing I know to do right now because if he gets up

there and gives them a medal for being *dead* while both of them are sitting right here in this office *alive* and the newspapers ever find out, he'll be the laughingstock . . . Get out of here and hurry," he shouted. "By God, step on it!"

Then Sergeant King went bounding out of the front door like he was in a race or something, and then the Lieutenant started in on us again but couldnt think of much to say, and finally just stopped with his finger up in the air and said, "Get in that office there and shut the door. And stay there! And if anybody comes in, you tell them you're John Jones and Jack Smith—do you understand that now?"

"They's just one thing," I said. "About them medals . . ."

"Get in there!" he yelled.

So me and Ben went in the other office and he slammed the door shut, and we waited in there for a while, and then in a little bit there was another commotion in the outside office; and we heered the Captain say, "I dont believe it!" and then the door flung open again and the Lieutenant was pointing at us and the Captain was staring at us, and the Captain said, "Are you sure?" and the Lieutenant said, "Sure, I'm sure!"

"What's your names?" the Captain asked us.

"I'm John Jones and this here is Jack Smith, sir," I said.

Then the Captain looked at the Lieutenant and said, "Listen, Jim, if you're trying to pull my leg, it'll be the last time because that's carrying joking too far, joking over the dead . . ."

"Dead! There they sit, right there, and they aint any more dead than you are! That idiot gave those names just because I told him to say that. That's them all right. Sergeant King identified them!"

"Well, I'm beginning to think that dont mean too much,"

the Captain said. "Seems like Sergeant King identified them the other time too . . ."

"It's them," the Lieutenant said. "I remember that long moronic-looking one myself. I'm trying to keep them hid back here until we figure something out. I'm telling you, Tom, if the General gets up there and gives them medals . . ."

"Well, come on," the Captain said. "Let's get something done about it. . . ."

Then he went out and the Lieutenant started to shut the door, but then he looked back at us and yelled out again, "If you move from there, I'll have you shot!" and slammed the door, and Ben turned white as a ghost again.

"Look," I said. "Things will be all right once they calm down a bit. Maybe we'll get to see the General and I'll talk to him and . . ."

"I wish I had never got off that plane," Ben said. "I wish I'd stayed on it even if it killed me." He set there with his face in his hands, then set up blinking his eyes while outside in the other office they kept going at each other, running around and banging doors, with Ben jumping every time one banged, and it got right tiresome after a while. We set there and listened, and then I rolled a cigarette and smoked it, and then there was some more talking, and after a little bit I heered the front door slam again and the Lieutenant say, "What did the General do?"

And then I heered Sergeant King's voice say: "Sir, I reported to the General and informed him as to the situation and advised him that under the very unusual circumstances that he desist in presenting posthumously the medals to the supposed deceased as it has been found that, completely contrary to all intelligence reports to the contrary, that . . ."

"By God!" the Lieutenant said. "Answer my question! Has he already presented the medals or not?"

"Yessir," Sergeant King said. "He had already done it."

"Lord," the Captain said. "Lordy Lord. What did he say then?"

"He said he would be right down, sir. He said for you to hold the men here and not let anybody else know about it . . ."

"What else?"

"He went on to say, sir, that if the news did leak out that he had presented medals to two airmen for bravery beyond the call of duty when those two airmen were sitting right up here fat and healthy in this Orderly Room, he would court-martial every man he could get his hands on in this squadron. . . ."

"And he aint kidding," the Lieutenant said. "He would eat us alive. Did he add anything further, Sergeant?"

"He said, 'So help him, God!' sir."

"And may the same be applied to you, Sergeant," the Lieutenant said. "If you have an excuse, I would advise you to start working it out fully right now."

And they fussed and fumed some more like that in the next room, so finally I took a seat in the Captain's chair and smoked another cigarette; and then in a little bit I heered this car outside and got up and went to the window in time to see the General come busting out of the back seat, heading for the Orderly Room. Then I heered the door slam again and heered him stomping in saying, "What do you mean, they arent dead!"

"Sir," the Captain said. "There's been a slight mix-up and . . ."

"A slight mix-up," the General bellowed. "You mean I'm

in a position where two privates have got me over such a barrel that all they got to do is open their mouths to somebody or just show themselves in public and I'm made the biggest joke in the Air Force, and you call it a slight mix-up! Where are they anyhow? It would be right interesting just to look at two people who practically hold my career in their hands and make me look like the biggest fool that ever graduated from the Point—where are they anyhow?"

"They're in the next office, sir," the Captain said. "We kept them hid back there."

And then the door opened and the General stood there and looked at us a minute, and then the door slammed again, and then they started going through the same stuff again with Sergeant King talking and the Captain talking and the Lieutenant talking, until they finally quieted down a bit, and the General said, "Sergeant, see if you can get General Pollard on the phone for me. I've done him many a favor and maybe this time he'll help me out, because God knows, this is one time I'm going to need it. If we can just handle this thing right, we might be able to work out of it somehow . . . at least, we better, and I'm telling you all that. Get General Pollard on the phone and I'll talk to him, and then if these boys are willing, I think I might handle it . . . Step on it," he said, "We've got to move fast."

So they talked a while longer and then the General went to the phone up in the other side of the building where we couldnt hear him and talked up there, and after a bit they quieted down some. So then we didnt hear nothing but mumbling for a while, and then all of a sudden the door started opening real easy and soft which made Ben jump even more than when they was slamming as I guess he had got kind of used to the noise by then; and the General come

in with some overcoats over his arm, the others following behind, and he seemed just as pleasant as you could ask. He come in smiling and saying, "Well, boys, it looks like we had a little mix-up, doesnt it?" and then he chuckled a little bit, and said it again, and chuckled some more; and then he said, "Yessir, we sure did, but I guess we can straighten things out, cant we? You can straighten most things out if everybody co-operates—that's all we need really, just a little bit of co-operation, isnt it?"

Then Ben snapped out, "Yessir," and the General said, "Well, I'm mighty glad to hear you feel that way about it because if you didnt, there could be all kinds of trouble. You boys could even get court-maritaled and sent off to prison, and neither one of you would like that, would you? No sir, so that's the reason we're going to straighten things out. I'm going to co-operate with you and you're going to co-operate with me."

"Sho," I said. "And I'm mighty glad you feel that way about it because everybody has been arguing and taking on so much you couldnt make much sense out of them . . ."

"Well, of course they were all right surprised and *happy too* having you boys back, and they just didnt think how you boys might feel about it, you know."

"Yessir," I said. "That's just what I was telling Ben. I said when everybody got calmed down it would be all right."

"Yes," the General said. "I'm glad you told Ben that. But right now, we've got to get started on straightening this mess out, havent we? Come on now, I want you to put these overcoats on and pull them way up over your heads, and I'm going to open the trunk of the car, and when I say 'Go,' I want you boys to run and jump in the trunk, you see. That's for precaution, just to make sure. Then I'll close it up and we'll

go to see General Pollard. Is that all right with you boys?"

"Yessir," Ben said. "We'll do just what you say."

And I felt the same because he was a right nice fellow. I figgered it would be hot down in the bottom of that car, but Ben was willing, so I didnt say anything. So then Sergeant King went outside to see if anybody else was around and he come back and said there warnt, and then the General poked his head out the door too, and then come back and said, "Okay now, run for it!" and give Ben a little shove out the door.

So Ben run out and hopped in the back of the car, and then the General started to give me a shove, but I held up a minute to speak with him.

"Run for it," he said. "What are you standing there for?"

"They's something I want to see you about," I said. "Ben, he takes a lot of stock in them medals and things and . . ."

"Look," the General said. "We can talk about that later, cant we? Hurry up before somebody sees him out there! Hurry now!"

"Well, I dont want to talk about it around Ben, you see. I mean he's kind of particular sometimes and might not like it, but I was thinking that if you could give us them medals you had, Ben would be mighty grateful and . . ."

"My God!" the General said. "I've been put over a barrel before but I never had anybody hold me over one the way you do! Hurry up now before somebody sees him and spoils the whole thing!"

"You see, Ben, he kind of figgered with all the rest of them getting one for pulling each other out of that plane, me and him . . ."

"All right!" he yelled. "All right! He'll get the medal. I'll

see to that myself. What do you want me to do now, swear to it? Get going now, for God's sake!"

So I took off then and run and jumped in the back of the trunk myself. And then they slammed down the top of it with it so dark inside that we couldnt even see each other, and then they drove off with the tire and the jack bouncing around in the back and banging up against us every time we moved so that it warnt very comfortable, but I didnt mind as I got right excited over how surprised Ben would be to get that medal. And I was right glad he couldnt see my face there in the dark, because I know it would have give it all away for sho.

24

Anyhow, I finally got comfortable in the back even though it was too little for me so I had to get kind of doubled up in it; but I managed to hold the jack down under my feet and get a grip on the tire so it wouldnt bounce no more, and finally got right comfortable and got to sleep for a while, and I guess we must have slept for a long time because by the time we stopped, it was already dark outside. Somebody pulled up the top of the trunk and all I could see

was a bunch of men standing around with flashlights and things, but I knowed we was out in the woods somewhere because I could smell it and could hear some frogs and crickets chattering away. And then I recognized the General behind one of the flashlights saying, "All right, boys, here we are. Come on and hop out now."

So I crawled out and said, "Come on, Ben. Get up and see where we are *now*," and he stirred and sat up and looked around at all the flashlights and things, blinking his eyes and looking worried again. So I said, "Come on, hop out, we're going to get everything straightened out now, like the General says," and he finally clumb out, looking this way and that, and I followed him, feeling all stiff from being curled up inside the trunk for so long. We looked around at things, trying to make them out—I didnt know where we was, though, except that it was out in the woods. There was another car parked down the way with its lights on, and over next to it was this old cabin with the roof of the porch leaning down, looking like nobody lived in it. Then I made out some of the others standing around—there was the General and the Captain and the Lieutenant and Sergeant King, and another fellow with a bunch of papers under his arm, and another older man standing over by the side with a star on his collar. They was all walking around holding flashlights and talking low, their feet crunching over pine needles and sticks and things. I looked at the other older man for a second and then the General said, "Boys, this is General Pollard. I've told him about our little mix-up and he's offered to help us out. We better go in the cabin now because we've got a lot of papers to fill out, and then I think everything is going to be all right." Then he looked at General Pollard

and said, "We'll just have to find a good place to send them."

"Well, dont worry about that," General Pollard said. "I know this place at Fort Jennings in Georgia, and Colonel McGee will handle it nicely."

So they talked a while longer and the fellow kept typing, and I wanted to get the General off to the side so Ben couldnt hear, but he kept going over to the typewriter and getting these papers for us to sign, and kept explaining them to us. "This one is a letter to your folks that says you are on a se-cret mission and not dead after all, but that they shouldnt mention it to anybody because of the secret *mission*. And this is a document which swears that you have never been stationed on your last base and have never been under my command and have never been in an airplane crash in your life, and this other one has your new serial number on it; and this other one is a document whereby you swear never to tell anything at all about all this because we're listing it as Top Secret, and you're liable to be court-martialed if you do, you see. You boys understand that now?"

"Yessir," Ben said, and he signed, and I done the same.

"You're sure that's clear now?"

"Yessir," I said. "There's just one thing I . . ." but then I stopped because Ben was setting there.

Anyhow, he went on that way for the longest sort of time with us signing papers just as fast as he could get them out of the typewriter, and it looked like I warnt going to have a chance to talk with him at all. But when he brought out the last batch and left them with us and went out on the porch, I got a hold of the pen first and signed mine before Ben, and followed him out there. And this time I got him aside where nobody else could hear, and I said, "What about them

medals, General? Like I was telling you, Ben takes a lot of stock in medals and parades and things like that, and he's real upset now and I was thinking . . ."

And he turned and stared at me for a while, but then he said, "Oh, yes, I did say I would see about that, didn't I? Okay, I dont guess it will hurt anything. I might as well do that too. Like I say, if you boys co-operate with me about this and keep your mouths shut, I'll co-operate with you. You just wait here a minute."

So then he went over to the typewriter and whispered something to the fellow and then come back to me and said, "I'm getting him to type up the papers a little different leaving out the deceased and so on, you know. I still have the medals in my pocket; I'll just slip them to you and you can give one to Ben and you can get the papers as soon as he finishes with them. Just dont let anybody know about it, though. They might not understand and . . . well, just dont . . ." And then he started fumbling in his pocket for the medals, shaking his head and saying, "Boy, you do drive a hard bargain, but I kind of agree with you in a way. I dont believe in doing anything halfway myself. . . ."

And then he was trying to hand the medals to me, but I didnt take them. I said, "Yessir, that's what I figgered. That's the reason I was wondering if you couldnt do it up right for Ben because he takes a lot of stock in things like that. I know he would appreciate it. I was thinking . . ."

"Do what now?"

"I mean like you give them out to Lieutenant Bridges and them. You know, standing up there stiff and saying a lot of words and things like that. . . ."

"You mean you want me to *present* them? Out here in the woods? You . . . ?"

"Well, it's just Ben is always talking about medals and things, you know, and he'd kind of like it done up right and all."

And then he kind of seen what I meant and I think he kind of got excited about it too after thinking it over for a bit because it looked like to me he just started quivering all over, so to speak. And he finally give a kind of deep breath and said, "Okay, I guess I've got it coming. I know when I've had it, boy. Now if I didnt have twenty-eight years in and my whole career, right now I would . . . well, never mind. Okay, you go in there and sneak Ben out here and we'll all go over yonder behind a tree and . . ."

"That's good," I said. "I was thinking maybe we could turn one of these cars around here so we could get some light, and they could line up over yonder and everybody could kind of stand at attention and everything."

And he kind of liked that idea too because he just started to quivering all over again. He stared at me and thought about it and kind of rolled his eyes up in the air thinking about it, and started biting on his lips and everything, and finally he said, "All right, I'll do it. I'll do it. I'll do it, by God!" And then he went back over to the fellow at the typewriter and said, "Corporal, get those things typed up, and when you finish with them, come out here with them. Sergeant King, get one of these cars turned around so the lights are shining up this way, and then get out and stand at attention."

"Do what, General?"

And then the General he quivered some more, looking at Sergeant King, and said in this low voice, "Just do what I said and quit standing there like an idiot. If it hadnt been for you, this whole thing . . ." but then he stopped, because

he had thought of something else. He called out, "Captain, you and the Lieutenant come out here a minute!" Then when they come out, he took a deep breath and said, "You men stand over there at attention."

"Do what, General?"

And then the General got right up in his face and said to him, "Look, if you dont mind, I dont want anybody else *questioning* me. You just get over there like I said. And Corporal, you get over there too. And if you dont mind, dont say 'Do what' to me; just get over there." And then he stood there a little bit, quivering some more while they got all lined and really done a nice job on it. Once he got the idea, he was just as excited about it as I was. He finally turned to me again and said, "You do understand why we dont have a band here, dont you? I hope this will be all right for you and Ben. You do understand how it was that it slipped my mind to bring the band along, dont you?"

"Sho," I said. "I wouldnt worry about it none. This'll be all right, I think."

"Well, I hope so. I hope it lives up to Ben's standards all right." And then he stood there breathing real deep and said, "Now if you'll just run along and quit standing there *looking* at me, I think I can handle the rest of the arrangements all right. There's not anything else you can think of at the moment, is there?"

"Well, I was thinking that maybe if you could get General Pollard to stand over there then we would have *two* generals and . . ."

And that kind of got him I think because he hadnt thought of it himself. He kind of swelled up and said, "By God!" and stood there staring at me some more, but finally once he seen the idea, he settled back down again real good. He said, "All

right; if you'll just get away from me now . . . If you'll just go on in and get Ben, and get away from me now, I think I can probably handle the rest myself."

So I went on in even though I did have one other pretty good idea about how they could all probably hum one of them marches so that Ben would have something to walk in time to, but I didnt say nothing else about it because you could tell he was already bothered about not having thought up a lot of stuff that I had, and I didnt want him to feel no worse about it. I went on in to where Ben was and he couldnt figger out what was going on, and I got a kick out of it too. The General was outside trying to get Sergeant King to do things right; he was saying, "If you say 'Do what, General,' to me one more time, Sergeant . . . And would you mind getting that stupid look off your face? And when we get through with this goddamned ceremony, would you mind stepping inside there too? Because I think I'm going to want you to sign a few papers too. Yessir, I think I will. Do you hear that, Corporal—as soon as this is over, you type up a few papers for Sergeant King too, only let's dont use that title any more—we'll just make it *Private* King from here on out."

Anyhow, Ben kept looking this way and that saying, "What's going on out there? What's the matter?"

"You just wait," I said. "The General is fixing up a surprise for you."

"Everybody's outside," Ben said. "Maybe we better get out there. Maybe . . ."

"No, not yet. The General will call us when he's ready. He said for you to just wait here."

But it took a little while because at first General Pollard didnt quite understand what he was supposed to do, and

when the General said, "Vernon, would you mind?" he said, "Now, by God, Jack, I'll do a lot of things for you but if you expect me to stand at attention out here in the woods for a couple of privates . . ." but the General said, "Look, Vernon, I know how you feel, God knows, but if you'll help me out this time and let me get this over with, someday I'll make it up to you. I really will because that fellow has got me where he wants me and . . ."

And they kept talking about it for a while until General Pollard understood where he was supposed to stand, and agreed on it, and it worked out mighty good that way, and *looked* mighty good too with them all standing at attention. And when the General called out, "All right, come on out here and get it!" Ben was so surprised, he didnt know what to do with himself.

"Go ahead, Ben," I said. "You're supposed to strut up to the General there and he's going to give you a medal!"

"I dont believe it," he said. "I . . ."

But then the general bellowed at him right loud, "Come on out, goddamnit! Come on out and get it!" and you should have seen the way Ben looked then. His eyes kind of brightened and his face lit up, and then he throwed out his scrawny little old chest, and started strutting. He went down the steps with me marching next to him, holding his head straight forward like you are supposed to, but still darting his eyes this way and that, he was so surprised. I walked along with him across the yard and past the car, going something like a drum with my mouth. I said, "Rat-tat-ta-tat" kind of clicking my tongue so he would have something to walk in step with, and he prissed along that way until he got up to the General, and then he stopped and throwed him a right snappy salute, and the General quivered a bit and give

212

him one back, and everybody was standing there at attention, and it was something to see too. The Corporal held the flashlight and the General read off all the things on the paper, saying how we had pulled each other out of the burning wreckage of the airplane and how proud the Air Force was of us, and how we reflected glory and everything, and then he got through that and ended up by pinning the medals on our chests, and Ben was pretty swelled up by the time it was over. We shook hands with everybody and they congratulated us, and finally the General said, "Well, if that's all you can think of you want from me, I guess that about does it. Hop in the car over there and the driver will run you out to the airport where I've got a special plane waiting for you."

"Well, hit was mighty nice," I said. "And we do want you to know how much we appreciate it."

But he didnt answer, just stood there a minute and then turned away and started for the house again. But then he seen Sergeant King kind of standing around over behind the house where he had been for a while, and stopped and bellowed at him, "I see you, by God! You're not going to get out of anything hiding back there. Come on in here and sign these papers! Because you're going with them every step of the way, and you just better thank the Lord Almighty that Private is the lowest rank I can think of at the moment."

So everything worked out pretty good that way and when I heered Sergeant King was going to get to go along with us, I felt pretty good about things. Me and Ben went out and sat in the car. And after a little bit, Sergeant King come out and got in the car too, and the driver started off; and I felt so lively and everything, I reached over and popped Ben on the back and said, "See there, Ben, you got a medal

after all, and aint even dead besides. And you were right about the Air Force too because the medals . . ."

"Air Force?" the driver turned around and said. "You fellows are in the Infantry now."

"Infantry!" Ben said.

"That's right, buddie. As of now, you fellows are transferred. Your new uniforms are in the back and as soon as we get to the airport, you'll have to change. Yessir, you're in the Infantry now. You've had it, buddie."

And then Ben looked at me with this big smile spreading across his whole face, and he reached up and touched the medal hanging off his chest, and said, "Well, I'll be danged, we made the Infantry after all," and seemed mighty happy about it. And Sergeant King was too, I think; he set there staring out the window for the longest sort of time, not saying a word, like he couldnt believe it almost. And when Ben said, "Yessir, we're just like the Three Musqueteers; I'll bet we'll stay in the same outfits and everything all the time we're in the Infantry!" Sergeant King got so excited over it, he set there and quivered, just like the General had done, all the way to the airport.

MAC HYMAN was born in Cordele, Georgia, in 1923, and spent most of his life there until he went away to school. He attended North Georgia College, a military school, and then Duke University and Auburn. He was drafted in 1943, passed the Air Corps examinations and finally ended up a navigator. He went overseas with one of the first B-29 outfits as a lieutenant in photo-navigation, first to Saipan and then to Guam. Before the war was over he had flown about twenty-three combat missions over Japan.

After World War II he returned to Duke and began to write. Also at this point he got married to his childhood sweetheart. Soon he was living in New York City, working for a time as a shipping clerk in a book store, and then in St. Augustine, Florida, where both he and his wife tried teaching school. He was broke when his first child was born, so he re-enlisted in the Air Force and ended up in Houston, Texas.

It was then that he began writing *No Time for Sergeants*. He continued working on it after he got out of the Air Force and while attending Columbia University under the G.I. Bill, and finally finished it down in Georgia on his father's farm.